WHO?

Iron
Dinosaurs

By the same author:

Symphony in Steam

LAST STEAM LOCOMOTIVES OF THE WORLD
  Twilight of Steam
  Masterpieces in Steam
  Steam Safari

For Jonathan...

Last Steam Locomotives of the World:

South East Asia

Iron Dinosaurs

Written and photographed

by

COLIN GARRATT

BLANDFORD PRESS

Poole   Dorset

Blandford Press Ltd,
Link House, West Street,
Poole, Dorset BH15 1LL

First published 1976

Colour section printed in 4-colour lithography
by Colour Reproductions Ltd, Billericay.
Text set in Baskerville 10/11 point
by Woolaston Parker Ltd.
Printed and bound by Butler & Tanner, Frome

ISBN 0 7137 0670 8

Contents

This volume contains a selection of locomotives from the following countries.

Country	Railway Company	Gauge
INDONESIA (JAVA, SUMATRA)	PJKA – Indonesian State Railways	600 mm
	,, ,,	3 ft 6 in.
	,, ,,	4 ft 8½ in.
	PNP XX State Sugar Plantations	700 mm
TAIWAN (JAPANESE NATIONAL RAILWAY CLASSES)	TGR Taiwan Government Railways	3 ft 6 in.
PHILIPPINES (NEGROS ISLAND)	The Insular Lumber Co.	3 ft 6 in.
	The Hawaiian Philippine Co.	3 ft 0 in.
	Ma-Ao Sugar Central	3 ft 0 in.

Author's Note

This volume could not have been compiled without the warm-hearted generosity of the Indonesian people, be they officials in private companies, staff of the PJKA or simply individuals. I write these words as a tribute to them all.

The text may seem a little wild and florid in style, this is simply the way in which it was written; nowhere have I exaggerated or deviated from the truth in any way. Having made this point, I wish to emphasise that what has been written is in no way meant to be disrespectful, neither is it an attempt to blandly poke fun at a developing nation. The observations that I have made will, I know, be accepted in good part by the Indonesian people – for their sense of humour about life in general and their own particular predicament is boundless.

All photographs in this book were taken with a Praktica Camera using Pentacon Lenses on Agfa CT 18 reversal film.

Lectures and colour shows based on this series are being given nationally. All details available from: Monica Gladdle. Tel: (05374)–5179

Introduction

Nowadays most of the world's surviving steam engines are both sane and rational in their appearance. It is inevitable that as the steam locomotive's world status diminishes the residue of types will become increasingly uniform in design and function, with modern 'mixed traffic' classes, manufactured in the light of latter day world experience and devoid of much traditional lineage, predominating; sadly, such engines can look much the same the world over.

Few would deny that modern utilitarian engines are interesting, of course they are, but their overall sanity and uniformity can at times become a little oppressive. The steam engine's capacity to look both quaint and bizarre is, I believe, one of its greatest attributes – the creations of Disney and Emett which so captivate both the young mind and adult imagination are evidence enough of this, but in the real world such engines, though once widespread are becoming extremely difficult to find. The modern steam giant is an intense mass of seething energy, symbolising power and animation, but this is only one aspect of the subject for the steam engine can also be an outlandish creation possessing more than a hint of the ridiculous.

For many years I had dreamed of bringing together a collection of engines which would not only rival Emett's prolific imagination, but which would also show some of the more delicious aspects of old, rustic-looking machines – some of which can be traced back to early evolutionary forms. There is only one concise area in which such expression can be found – South East Asia and the Philippine Islands. As can be imagined, the engines contained in these pages have a pungent atmosphere and it is this that I have tried to capture on the printed page, both by mode of photography and written word. I have hand picked the engine types in an endeavour to provide an overall sensation of various kinds of locomotives now virtually extinct;

9

in brief, I have made a religion of these engines with the faith that the examples chosen will, by their complete detachment from normality, inspire the imagination.

This book does not attempt to cover all the surviving steam locomotives of this geographical area. Had it done so, it would not have provided the necessary contrast with its companion volumes in the 'Last Steam Locomotives of the World' series. However I have depicted the engines chosen in a wide range of moods. Throughout the world, there are thousands of different designs still active; to record them all in their infinite detail and differences would be impossible (and indeed not really necessary).

Whether one's adventures with steam engines be orientated towards the historical or aesthetical, vivid personal encounters are inevitable, especially in strange lands, and in this volume I have written of my experiences in an effort to both back up the photographs and recapture also the atmosphere of the living moment, since it is my belief that the study of steam locomotives can be as much a personal, emotive experience as it is an important exercise in historical research.

But how will the reader respond to the engines in this book? Ever since research revealed the existence of these freakish veterans they formed for me a glorious mixture of dreams and ambition which could only be consummated by a visit to see and record the engines at first hand. Surely, I decided, they are all 'dinosaurs', but the title was particularly inspired by the engines of the Insular Lumber Company on Negros – probably the most incredible of them all! The dice of life lands in different ways, but the luck that led me to discover these veritable gems was a fortune indeed: it was none other than an act of grace to have been able to see, ride upon and work with, the locomotives pictured and discussed within these covers.

I hope when turning the pages that ensue the reader will be immersed in the joys of studying these battered remnants of

Victoriana: included are some epic mainliners, along with lesser known engines located in remote quarries, sugar plantations and logging railways. The glorious landscape, often volcanic, will be sensed rather than seen in detail, pride of place being given always to the colourful and vibrant forms of the engines themselves. Thus I hope to have epitomised the quaint, the hideous, the bizarre and the romantic as well as the very stench of iron, and set these monstrous freaks against the backcloths of their everyday world.

Many willing hands paved the way for my journeys in tracking down the dinosaurs and it is my privilege to thank the following for their various contributions towards this work.

Firstly the PJKA authorities and individuals; A. D. & S. Siregar, R. D. Silitonga, M/s Soetarmin and Moetjono of Madiun, Jwono Djenawi, Mr Sama of Cirebon and S. Sumana. On the Indonesian industrial plantations; A. Damanik of Bah Djambi, M/s Soenarno and Soetrisno of PG Pesantren, Antonius Arifin of PG Purwodadi, and R. Hisam Maugkoeprajitno and family of PG Meritjan. To the Taiwan Government Railways for facilities granted during a time of political difficulty and also to Mr Chong Chang of Chia Yi. At the Insular Lumber Co., my sincere thanks to Angel S. Tiangson Jr, Conrad, Simplicio N. Moreno and family and Ignacio B. Golez. At the Hawaiian Philippine Co., Mrs L. Arceo Samaniego, Mr and Mrs Caparros and family, Regino S. Acosta, Olimpio B. Gonzales, Felipe Gonzales and at Ma Ao Central to Agapito Corpez and Mr and Mrs Guillermo Araneta and family. Here in England, I acknowledge kind assistance from Sheila Ramsden, Mrs M. E. Warner, Brian Healey, Horace Gamble, Andrew Turk and of course, David Thornhill along with his monthly publication 'World Steam', obtainable from 124, Wendover Road, Stoke Mandeville, Bucks. Lastly, as ever, my greatest thanks to Judy Warner for her efforts on behalf of this volume.

Colin Garratt July, 1975

(1) The last 2-4-0 express passenger engines in the world are represented by this ailing Indonesian B50 Class engine built by Sharp Stewart of Manchester in the 1880's.

(2) 'Dragon 7' of the Hawaiian-Philippine Co working in the plantatio
This company officially refers to their locomotives as 'Dragons'.

on Negros Island. She is an o-6-o built by Baldwin of America in 1920.

(3) A multi-coloured veteran in the form of an Alco 2-6-0 of 1924 trundles
tender came from an old Baldwin 0-6-2.

er the metals of the Ma-Ao Sugar Central on Negros. Her decorative

(4) Dawn in the teak woods of Negros finds a priceless 3 ft 6 in. gauge 0-6-6-0 4-cylinder compound Mallet waiting to take logs down to the sawmill.

(5) As dawn breaks over Fabrica on Negros Isle, an old Lima 2-truck Shay raises steam for a day's tripping round the sawmill of the Insular Lumber Co.

(6)   One of the world's last Vertical Cylinder Shay engines, a 3-cylinder, 3-truck
design by Lima, ends her day's as Insular Lumber Co No 12.

(7) A historic study showing the last of the Indonesian 2-4-0s. On the
a Class B50 tender engine from Sharp Stewart of Manchester in 1

a splendid B13 Class Side Tank from Hanomag in 1885 seen alongside

(8)   Shimmering in the heat of blazing cane leaves Hawaiian-Philippin

Co's Dragon No 6, and trundles empties through the **plantations of Negros.**

(9) The world's last giant main line Mallets rot their way back to nature amid the tropical vegetation of Java. On the left is a PJKA Class DD52 2-8-8-0 along with an original American-built Class DD51 2-8-8-0.

(10) The last 0-4-2 express passenger engines in the world suffer a similar fate on Java. These 4 ft 8½ in. gauge engines of typical British appearance were built by Beyer Peacock of Manchester in the 1880's.

(11)   An old and unidentified Indonesian 0-4-2 Side Tank engine from the privately
owned Rejo-Agung Sugar Co lies abandoned amid encroaching vegetation.

(12) A rare scene depicting two enormous 4-cylinder Compound Mal
standing alongside a Class CC10 2-6-6-0T. They are pictured at

of both tender and tank varieties. On the left is a PJKA Class CC50 2-6-6-0
rut on the Cibatu – Cikajang line in Java.

(13)   The British delineation of this Manchester-built PJKA Class B50 2-4-0 is evide
Notice the logs on the tender and the antiquated 4-wheeled coaching stock.

she arrives at Madiun with a passenger train from Ponorogo.

(14) An excitingly decrepit Alco 2-6-0 of 1924 surrounded by su[...]
Islands.

...ane far out in the plantation of Ma-Ao Sugar Central, Negros, Philippine

(15) Three Taiwan Government Railways classes boil up outside the depo
DT580 2-8-0, CT 150 2-6-0 and DT650 2-8-2. These correspond with

Hsinchu on Taiwan's west coast main line. Left to right are Classes
Japanese National Railway Classes 9600, 8620 and D51 respectively.

(16) 'Bromo' named after an extinct Javan volcano is a 700 mm outside framed 0-8-0TT from Orenstein and Koppel in 1914. She is seen passing one of Java's magnificent flowering trees.

(17) Old Lima 3-truck Shay No. 12 of the Insular Lumber Co sprays the tropical surrounds with teak sparks as she proceeds to collect logs from the woods of Negros.

(18) Though in moribund condition this PJKA Class B51 4-4-0 eloqu
magnificent 2-cylinder compounds were sent to the Dutch East I

plays her Prussian ancestry. Built in both Germany and Holland these
·ly this century.

(19)   No 7, an 0-6-6-0 Compound Mallet from Baldwin and No 12, a 3-truck Vertical Cylinder Shay from Lima. Now almost freaks of evolution, the engines belong to the Insular Lumber Co, Negros, Philippines.

(20)   An active volcano forms the backdrop to this sunrise scene of an Alco 2-6-0 working one of the mountainous lines for Ma-Ao Sugar Central, Philippines.

(21) Colouring the night sky with fire, Shay No 10 of the Insular Lumber Co shuffles along between the sawmill and planing mill at Fabrica.

(22) Lima 3-truck Shay No 12 backs a splendid train load of teak log
to take them down to the sawmill at Fabrica.

g the mountain siding at Maaslud in readiness for Baldwin Mallet No 7

(23)   A tropical sunset adds further beauty to two rare survivors in J
nineteenth century 2-cylinder Compound 2-6-0 of 1895.

The PJKA Class D15 is a Klein-Linder axle 0-8-0T whilst the C12 is a

(24)   The beginnings of a typhoon are discernable in the dusky sky as Dragon Ne
Co's factory on Negros.

dles a load of sugar cane bound for the Hawaiian-Philippine

(25)　The PJKA's 60 cm stone railway in Northern Sumatra is a haven of antiquity in every respect. Here No 105 is seen approaching the cable operated incline with a trainload of stones from the river.

(26) With her diminutive waggons just loaded with stones PJKA No 105 sets off from the river bank. She was built by Orenstein and Koppel in 1920.

(27) The upper reaches of this stone railway in Sumatra are operated by No 106 a Dutch-built Ducroo and Brauns 0-6-0T of 1926 seen here trundling a loaded train through tropical forest.

(28) 'Dragon 6' a Baldwin 0-6-0 of 1920 threads a trainload of emp

r cars through the Hawaiian-Philippine Co's plantation.

(29) Bringing in the cane by night. Two of the delightful locos working
seen struggling into the factory yards with loads of cane. Left is 'W
Orenstein and Koppel of Germany.

700 mm gauge lines of P.G. Pesantren Sugar Co in East Java are 0-4-2T of 1901, whilst in the foreground is 'Smeroe' an 0-6-0TT by

(30) A historic scene depicting the world's last 4 ft 8½ in. gauge 0-4-engine has lain derelict for some 35 years. She was built by Be

passenger engine rotting away amid tropical vegetation in Java. This
...k of Manchester during the 1880's.

(31) A magnificent copper-capped 2-cylinder Compound 2-6-0T of PJKA Class C12 basks against a flaming sunset in Java.

(32)   As the moon lifts clear of cloud, 'Sriklandi', a 700 mm gauge outside framed 0-8-0TT from Orenstein and Koppel rumbles its way over the metals of the P. G. Redjo Sari in Java with a trainload of raw sugar.

(33)   Amid the locomotive graveyards of Java are found some of the v
Class DD52 2-8-8-0 whilst behind lies an older DD51 – an origin

giant Mallet 4-Cylinder Compound engines. On the left is a PJKA
ican-built Alco 2-8-8-0 of 1919.

(34) The awesome noise of a vertical cylinder Shay engine has to
from Lima, ends her days around the Insular Lumber sawmi

ard to be believed. Here, one of the last of the species, a 3-cylinder variant
abrica.

(35) With all the flamboyance of fairground engines on display, two of
during the milling season. The saddle tank is an 0-6-2 of 1924 whic
vintage.

waiian-Philippine Co's Baldwin built 'Dragons' go about their chores
inally came from Hawaii whilst the larger engine is an 0-6-0 of 1920

(36) Further invigorating an already colourful scene is 'Bromo' an Orenstein and Koppel 0-8-0TT of 1913. She is seen working at the P. G. Purwodadi Sugar Factory in Eastern Java. Notice the tender piled up with bagasse.

(37) This little Baldwin built 0-6-0 of the Hawaiian-Philippine Co was a forerunner of the larger 'Dragons' featured on other pages. The engine has 10 in. cylinders and was built in 1918.

(38) State flags commemorating Independence Day, semaphore signals and copped
      cap chimney do much to invigorate this Indonesian Class C12 2-cylinder
      Compound 2-6-0T – a variation of the simple Class C11 2-6-0s dating back to
      the 1870s.

(39) A typical Javan plantation scene showing a skyline of extinct volcar
'Dieng', is a 700 mm gauge 0-8-0TT by Orenstein and Koppel wor

g with the building up of mid-morning cloud. The engine, named
the P. G. Pesantren sugar fields.

(40)   A side wind buffets this veteran Class B50 2-4-0 of 1885 as she struggles along
with a passenger train from Madiun to Ponorogo. Notice her original chimney
now like a molten candle top.

(41) Another B50, this one of 1884, heads away from Madiun against a misty dawn. These are the world's last 2-4-0 express passenger engines and they date back to 1880.

(42)   A splendid piece of Americana depicting much of the atmosph
a wide range of colour tones this Alco 2-6-0 of 1924 sits well ag

ornate nineteenth century locomotive traditions of America. Sporting
rid sunset on Negros Island.

(43)   An oil-burning Baldwin o-6-o with rusty stovepipe chim

...ws a rake of loaded cane from a remote plantation siding on Negros.

(44) With the day's work finished two Indonesian veterans steam th
Klein-Linder axle 0-8-0T followed by a C12 2-6-0T of 1895.

back into the depot at Cepu. Leading is the last active PJKA D15

(45)   The displaced centre-line of a Shay's boiler is well illustrated here by this dawn study of a Lima built 3-truck Shay on Negros.

(46) Tingeing the river bed with the delicious aroma of teak smoke Shay No 12 trundles above the torrent at Minapasuk, site of the Insúlar Lumber Co's Base Camp on Negros.

(47) Until sufficient new season's bagasse has been dried and baled, se
to the fact is 'Dragon 7' a 1928 built Baldwin 0-6-0.

nes of the Hawaiian-Philippine Co burn oil. Giving good testimony

(48) A scene at Rangkasbitung showing two oil-fired PJKA Class B51 4-4-os boiling up outside the depot. These turn of the century engines show Prussian delineation.

(49) A 700 mm gauge 0-8-0TT hauling an overloaded train dramatically labours her way into the cane yard of the P.G. Meritjan Sugar Factory in East Java.

(50) The typhoon threatening for days finally breaks as the last of
Talisay-Silay Railway Alco built 2-6-0 of 1921 now working f

ay's sunlight scatters westwards. Seen awaiting the onslaught is an ex
-Ao Sugar Central, Negros.

(51) With servicing and crew changes completed, three Hawaiian-Philipp
Left to right: Nos 6, 5 and 4 all from Baldwin in 1920.

0-6-0s line up with full steam ready to commence night duties.

(52) Portrait of a Dinosaur! Perhaps the world's most fabulous st[...]
seen crossing the wooden Maaslud viaduct with a trainload [...]
tender piled up with freshly cut teak logs.

or is this Baldwin 3 ft 6 in. gauge 4-cylinder Compound 0-6-6-0 Mallet
the Insular Lumber Sawmill at Fabrica. Notice her gloriously lettered

(53) A PJKA Class B51 4-4-0 gaily decked with Independence flags peeps out of a
decrepit depot in Java with a Swiss designed Class C27 4-6-4T in the rear.

(54) The last PJKA D15 0-8-0T receives attention at Cepu depot in northern Java.

(55)   Few railways in the world can offer such thrilling sights as an American
Shay engines. Both are evolutionary developments from the conventiona
Maaslud exchange siding in the mountains of Negros.

-6-6-o Mallet standing alongside one of the last Vertical Cylinder
m locomotive. These two gems, bathed in fire, are seen at the

(56)   A Japanese Pacific working on the Taiwan Government Railw.
This rakish thoroughbred of the TGR Class CT270, is to the de

coast main line is seen outside the Chia Yi depot in southern Taiwan.
the Japanese National Railway's C57.

(57) An ancient PJKA Class CC10 2-6-6-0 Mallet tank engine heads the afternoon passenger train between Cibatu and Cikajang in central Java. She was built by Hartmann of Germany in 1905.

1. Indonesia: The Living Museum

When a zoologist reconstructs the bones of early creatures, he feels a tremendous curiosity about how the living specimen looked. Over the last century, the remains of countless extinct animals have been unearthed and reconstructed; fascinating and almost unbelievable creatures embracing early species of birds, mammals and, of course, the great dinosaurs. Tirelessly, intrepid zoologists have undertaken expeditions to remote areas and, bone by bone and tooth by tooth, have made painstaking reconstructions of a lost age. The world has gasped incredulously at their discoveries and, like the zoologist's, our imaginations have been enlivened by the mysteries of the pristine world. But it has not all been clinical retrospection, for the scientist has dreamt of discovering living examples – perhaps on some remote island, or tract of land where time has stood still and the magnificent creatures of old live on.

Future generations might regard the disappearance of the steam locomotive from the world's railways as a quirk of evolution comparable to the loss of the mighty dinosaur. Already most of the steam epoch's pleasures, both great and small, are gone and ever increasingly standardised forms of locomotive are bringing the steam age rapidly to its conclusion; the modern steamologist yearns to see those inanimate museum pieces spring to life.

When I first heard of the fantastic collection of antiquated types still operating on the far eastern islands of Java and Sumatra, I was told that some of the forms there could be traced back to the earliest days of the steam age itself! Subsequent research revealed that the Indonesian State Railways (PJKA) have less than 900 steam engines on their books and well under half are active at any given time. Seventy different classes, many of nineteenth century origin, are in existence, and many of the extant types owe their origins to builders whose

93

names have long since become a revered part of railway history. Moreover, I learned that outside the State railways confines, the vast palm-oil plantations of Sumatra and the widespread sugar fields of Java were said to be alive with steam engines of various shapes and colours. In metaphor, the two islands had become another 'Galapagos' having attracted attention from steamologists the world over.

It has been widely believed that 2–4–0 express passenger engines have long since been extinct so the reader can imagine my elation on discovering the 95-year-old, Manchester-built Sharp Stewart engines in Java. Another marvellous discovery, equally British in appearance was the related 0–4–2 tender engines; although these were found to be in badly decaying condition, having not turned a wheel for some 30 years, they do provide evidence of a fundamental type of early locomotive and furthermore, are surviving examples from Indonesia's old standard gauge network.

A later relation of these two types was the 4–4–0, represented on Java by two excitingly different classes. From the main stem of locomotive evolution sprang various offshoots, one of the most notable being the Mallet; the last big Mallet tender engines in the world plying their way daily through the volcanic mountains of West Java. In maximum contrast, diminutive steam tram engines, British-built in the nineteenth century, trundle along the roadsides and over cross-country branches – sometimes working turnabout with 0–4–0 tender engines. The only 0–4–0 tender engines most of us have ever seen are represented by old clockwork train-sets – a figment of the toy manufacturers' imagination, but in Indonesia these engines provide substance to fantasy and remain an enormous local asset. These are but a few of the treasures in a land where copper cap chimneys and burnished brass domes still gleam in the sunshine and where the magical atmosphere of a nineteenth century steam railway can still be felt in all its authenticity.

That such a glorious situation exists is tempered by tragic operating conditions in which a lack of facilities and trained personnel has played havoc with all but the very best main line expresses. Many of the steam dowagers would have gone long ago were it not for the multitude of diesel engines lying idle awaiting repairs. A desperate fuel shortage, be it wood, coal or oil has, in many districts completely stopped services with lines being closed indefinitely. No time-tables are issued for secondary routes, and even when trains are running, their times can vary greatly from day to day – the travelling populace, along with their wares and livestock, simply squatting around the station area until the train deems to arrive. The situation has become increasingly worse over the last year or two and now maintenance has become so great a problem that even given the fuel, mechanical failure on an engine might equally paralyse services since many depots only possess one steamable engine.

Recent political disruptions have done much to run down the country's economy, whilst overpopulation is rife; nearly eighty million on Java alone; an island only 600 miles long by less than 100 miles wide; 51,000 square miles in all! Inevitably the people are poor, many desperately so, but no one starves thanks to the frequent rains and a rich soil which provides abundant rice, vegetables and fruit. Chickens proliferate everywhere, be it city street, waterfront or kampong and provide the major protein source. The Indonesians seem to have a strange compulsion for continually moving about and this, combined with a thriving commerce – predominantly agricultural – means that the roads and villages are alive with movement; human beings, ox-drawn carts, animals and cycle rickshaws – the major form of urban travel – jostling for priority in the intense tropical heat with battered lorries and overladen buses whose clamorous horns top an incredible cacophony of sound. In this chaotic environment, the railway provides the vital lines of communication and in Java rail links proliferate. Apart from the two main lines, one running across the north and the other along the southern part of the island, the remainder are principally secondary branches serving rural peoples: it is upon such lines that many of the ailing iron-clad antiquities live on in borrowed time.

From the early seventeenth century until 1945, Indonesia as the Dutch East Indies was under Dutch colonial rule and the railways were developed under this regime from 1866 onwards. On Java one network was laid to standard gauge ($4 \text{ ft } 8\frac{1}{2} \text{ in.}$) by the Nederlands Indische Spoorweg Maatschappi (Nis) whilst the Staats Spoorwegan (SS) was laid to the now standard 3 ft 6 in. gauge. Both these concerns ordered their own engines and later some of the lines were laid to mixed gauge. While the major networks were built by these organisations, many smaller steam tram companies added interconnecting lines on which specially ordered engines ran.

No standard gauge has ever existed in Sumatra, the first railway built there being the 75 cm Atjeh Tramway in the far north. The rest of Sumatra's railways comprise three main systems all being to a common 3 ft 6 in. gauge but not connected. In the north, radiating from Medan, the famous Deli Railway built up a network from 1886 with some fine engines which still exist on those metals today. The other two are both Staats Spoorwegan (Sumatra); one the mountainous west coast system in the centre of the island and later, from 1914 onwards, the south Sumatra system.

During World War II the Japanese invaded Indonesia, occupied it and imprisoned the Dutch. Immediately they began looting Java's standard gauge equipment and sent it to Manchuria where the retreating Chinese had taken all the railway equipment with them. The eventual outcome of this was a unified gauge in Indonesia; a portent towards future operational efficiency. Both the Deli system in Sumatra and the Javan (SS) had a limited amount of narrow gauge track though all that remains today is the 60 cm stone line discussed in the following chapter.

The war's end brought terrible upheavals in the country's internal affairs; post colonial independence being declared on 18 August 1945 when the Javan Railways were officially brought under State control; but many troubles were to beset the land until a United Nations action finally resolved independence from the Dutch in 1949. In 1963, Sumatra's railways were incorporated into the State enterprise, which since 1945 had been known as the PNKA. Recently these initials were adjusted to PJKA – Perusahaan Jawatan Kereta Api or Indonesian State Railways.

Germany, with her prolific locomotive building capacity, provided the majority of engines both mainline and industrial, though the Dutch, by courtesy of Werkspoor of Amsterdam, did contribute a fair number of mainliners with the less important firm Ducroo & Brauns in Weesp, building many smaller industrial types. However, some of the most worthwhile veterans running today have their origins in the British Victorian period; though in complete contrast, the last steam locomotive ever built in Britain – an 0–4–2ST from Hunslet of Leeds in 1971, was destined for a sugar factory in Java. American engines are virtually non-existent, a notable exception being the original giant 2–8–8–0 Mallets which were Alco thoroughbreds along with their subsequent European-built sisters.

One hopes that this book will whet the appetites of many would-be visitors and of the vintage engines the question must now be posed 'how long will it all last?' At present there can be no straight answer. Opinions in the country itself vary as from five years to twenty! Certainly the scheduled dieselisation programme is not going according to plan; many of the older diesels are lying idle for want of maintenance – in fact by the summer of 1974, apart from mainline expresses, the authorities were having the utmost difficulty in running any reliable and predictable service at all! What will eventually happen is anyone's guess, perhaps the present situation will go on indefinitely; perhaps things will improve – they could hardly be worse!

One conclusion may be that the government will be forced to close down many of their uneconomical rural branches, especially those which parallel roads, but a closer scrutiny suggests this move to be unlikely as the teeming population needs a cheap and comprehensive transport system. Apart from the very limited tricycle-rick-shaws, the railway, along with a motley array of dilapidated buses, is the only way of getting around. The ideal solution would be a hefty loan from the World Bank but to make any appreciable difference to the existing situation, the amount needed would have to be phenomenal since, apart from the investment required in track renewals, maintenance facilities, rolling stock and loco-motives, considerable staff training facilities would have to be implemented and, equally important, properly maintained.

Yet one feels instinctively that the present situation just cannot continue, something must happen. But possibly such a sentiment is conditioned by the thinking and progress of the affluent, sophisticated and technologically advanced nations. Here we are considering Indonesia, a land where things do not happen as if a magic wand had been waved. Until however Indonesia emerges as a modern nation soundly based on a thriving economy, the steamologist's ambitions at least will not be frustrated. He can still search through the graveyards where early forms of engines lie rotting their way into the earth, and then cross the mountain, or travel into the adjacent valley and find the same kind of machines puffing around with their whistles screaming and smoke stacks belching; still a living force in the land; his ultimate wish fulfilled. If only the great dinosaur expeditionists had been as fortunate in running down their quarry.

2. The Incredible Stone Railway

An incomprehensible flurry of Bihasa Indonesian came over the intercom, followed by a sedate and more appropriate, 'good morning ladies and gentlemen, welcome aboard our Merpati aircraft; flying time to Medan will be two and a half hours; would you fasten your seat belts now and refrain from smoking during take-off.' Minutes later we lifted up over Jakarta, Java's capital, and swung north-west, bound for the capital town of neighbouring Sumatra. The sun was barely risen, yet the cool atmosphere in the aircraft came as a welcome relief from the clinging humidity of late July.

A vast expanse of wild terrain obscured sometimes by cloud lay below: the great Sumatran forests, Savannah grasslands, sinuous rivers, smoking volcanoes; yellow dust roads fanning out like bands of gold across the predominantly green vista beneath. My preoccupation lay, however, with thoughts of the engines I hoped to see on North Sumatra's great steam hunting ground. The old Deli Railway – centred upon Medan – was, until recently, privately owned and still sported some vintage engines; research in England having pin-pointed such rarities as the 1884-built 0–4–2Ts – the original engines of the line, the turn of the century 0–4–4Ts bearing a hint of Johnson Midland Railway styling and the 1900-built 2–4–4Ts originally made as the 0–6–4Ts. In the more modern vein, I expected to see some lovely 1915-built Dutch 2–6–4Ts by Werkspoor and some of the curiously high-pitched 2–4–Ts from Hanomag in 1928 – an old wheel formation on a modern-looking engine! Apart from their main lines, the company also once owned some stone- and wood-carrying lines of 60 cm and 70 cm gauge respectively, though all that now survives is one remote stone line – allegedly better than anything Alice found in Wonderland; this stone line, above all, was the main object of my expedition.

I had been in Indonesia just a few hours, but shortly after

arrival in Medan I was to become initiated into a totally unpredictable mode of existence. Like a movie film speeded up, experiences were to rush upon me by the hour; life would never seem the same again.

My taxi from Medan airport was an old American car of prohibition period styling; it would have looked battered on a stock-car circuit! The doors were ill-fitting, windows jammed, seats split and with stuffing missing, the roof was buckled and – you have to believe it – there was even a gaping hole in the floor! The exhaust system was all but trailing along the ground, each bump in the road – and there were many – causing it to rattle and scrape. We sped through suburbs thronged with stalls and open-fronted shops which sold every conceivable commodity from motor-bikes to sliced papayas. Hordes of people intermingled in a sea of cars, rick-shaws, buses, cycles and ox-carts: never for more than a yard at a time were the roads clear and the blaring motor horns, exhaust fumes and excessive humidity induced a nausea guaranteed to dowse the ardour of the most hardy traveller.

During the journey a small boy jumped on to the taxi and, looking both pathetic and cunning, begged rupiahs, pointing to his open mouth indicating that he needed food – poor he undoubtedly was, but the starving act was cleverly designed to deceive the affluent tourist. But whatever their circumstances, Indonesians are on the whole a good-natured people, and their swarthy, brown faces break easily into radiant smiles.

Flanking the streets were dwellings ranging from modern tiled houses with ornately shuttered windows to crude thatch huts, their corrugated iron walls hugging the litter-ridden banks of the tepid, evil-smelling river; whilst homeless individuals lived without means of sanitation under market stalls, bridges and even under vehicles undergoing repairs in roadside yards. American pop-music of the 1950's howled out from cafes and street bazaars through cracked amplification systems and provided a perfect foil to the Sumatran capital.

My hotel, situated above the roar of a market place was like an oven; it had no air conditioning and no water until six that evening. Though exhausted, I found it too noisy to sleep and too hot to move about, whilst the ant-like activity all around banished anything but the most superficial concentration. Reminded however of my mission to observe some living legends of the old Deli Railway, I immediately hailed a gaily painted cycle-rick-shaw for a trip to the station. Over the previous 48 hours I had travelled some 8,000 miles in complete safety but the rick-shaw had barely got up the road before I was gripping the sides in sheer panic: the station lay a terrifying two kilometres away – I did not expect to make it. Whether the cycle boy was a genius or a madman is impossible to say, since apart from closing my eyes each time a collision seemed inevitable, it soon became obvious that rick-shaw riding is an art form. On one occasion when the driver seemed intent on ramming an approaching bus I was literally on the point of throwing myself clear; had it not been for a river on one side and a pair of lorries roaring along on the other I would doubtless have done so. The proverbial 'six inches to spare', saved the day, for little worse was suffered than a heap of grit deposited into my lap as the bus snarled past at unrepenting speed. In anguish I turned to look at the boy who returned a wide beaming smile which conveyed nothing.

Arriving at the longhouse, I marvelled at the antiquated machines all around me; at least one of all the Deli types was present but unfortunately only two engines were in steam. Indonesia's range of vintage steam engines are not an alien survival of an era long past but an intrinsic part of the present time. This may seem an obvious remark, but it is not until one actually arrives in the country that the engines, however antiquated can be seen as a perfect complement to the environment. It was to this environment that I had to respond, forgetting the sophisticated technology of developed nations and, like Alice herself, descend into another world; a world in which an ice lollipop or a cigar can be purchased for the equivalent of one half-penny!

From Medan, my train journey over the Deli main line to Tanjungbalai was a great revelation: the line, running in a south-easterly direction, is not far from the coast where, across the straits of Malacca, lies Malaya. The region's principal industry is palm-oil – important in the manufacture of soap and margarine – and the line passes through some vast plantations threaded with steam-operated narrow gauge railways. These lines radiate outwards from the modern palm-oil factories and run for miles deep into the plantations and are operated by some splendidly handsome 0–4–4–0T Mallets Dutch-built by Ducroo and Brauns. This industry, developed during the Dutch regime, now forms part of the PNP or National Plantation Corporation and is known as PNP *VI VII* – the numerals simply denoting the commodity – as distinct from Tobacco, Tea, Sugar and Rubber. The fruit, which is mostly delivered to the factory by rail, undergoes a complex manufacturing process, whilst the hard kernel shells are used as locomotive fuel; these, unlike bagasse – the natural waste product of sugar cane processing – are of a high calorific value. It is a characteristic sight at plantation engine sheds to see enormous heaps of grey-brown shells piled into line-side hoppers – I had seen locomotives fed on many things but never nutshells! Not all the plantations connect up with the Deli, some being completely self contained, but at Perlanaan – on the Deli main – a number of plantation lines converge and transfer ramps are provided to enable special 3 ft 6 in. gauge palm-oil waggons to be carried over the 70 cm gauge metals for loading at the factories.

At Perlanaan, ex Deli Railway No. 22, a delicious 2–4–4T (ex 0–6–4T) built by Hartmann of Germany in 1901, was on transfer duties trundling waggons from the nearby factory at Gunung Bayu: simmering on the narrow gauge metals was a Mallet and an 0–6–0 tender-tank engine – both from Ducroo and Brauns. Well over one hundred steam engines work this vast palm-oil industry, particularly around Siantar, a town at the end of a branch from Tebingtinggi on the Deli main line. It so transpired that a wish for reasonable hotel accommodation eventually obliged me to make Siantar a base and it was from here that I visited the stone railway.

The Deli Railways' quarry line, as it is known, lies at Gunung Kataren and although the Siantar – Tebingtinggi branch line passes close by, few trains stop; accordingly I was told to take the 'Siantar Express' bus service which passed a forest track leading directly to my objective. So, early one morning, armed with great anticipation, I arrived at the pick-up point at 6.00 a.m. to join a mass of people, baggage and animals, all waiting for the same bus. A convoy of lorries would be more appropriate for so great a crowd I mused, but was quietly assured, by means of some highly imaginative sign language, that I had no real cause for concern – everyone would get in!

The bus, all colours of the rainbow, was especially characterised by broken windows and a marked lack of usable seats; it arrived with horn blaring to clear some errant chickens – property of the people in front of the queue. The crowd swarmed over the vehicle; cycles and sacks of rice were hauled on top, baggage was roped to the sides whilst the two doors quickly swallowed up both chickens and humanity – myself included. I ended up sitting on the commodious lap of a large Indonesian lady with hens at my feet and a large sack of grain pressing against my left ear.

We set off at breakneck speed – whoever named it the 'Siantar Express' was not joking! During that 50-minute journey the horn blared out furiously as the bus was aimed along the narrow congested roads: the fact that I was completely unable to see out, though frustrating, was doubtless in the best interests of my nervous system. I could hardly believe my ears when the piped music began, but there sure enough, not nine inches above my head was a speaker – the gay rollicking songs which emanated could not have been more appropriate had they been specially composed for such a journey. But for all the discomfort and over excitements, I was amongst friends – although few could do more than wink and say 'Hello mister'.

Dutifully they set me down at my destination in the middle of a dense forest having pointed to a footpath through the trees. A resounding cheer went up as the bus moved away; a sea of smiling faces peered from every window: I was well into the forest before the combined sounds of music and the neurotically screaming engine of the bus finally died away.

The stone railway, though having all the qualities of an industrial line is actually operated by the PJKA and is, I understand, an important source of track ballast. It is a system blessed with that rustic antiquity so beloved by enthusiasts. Emerging from the trees, I was confronted by a primitive stone-crusher – a recent improvement since two years ago crushing was done manually by gangs of women and boys wielding tiny hammers! Alongside the crusher, at the head of a rake of diminutive waggons stood engine No. 106, a 1926-built 0–6–0T from Ducroo and Brauns of Weesp.

My arrival was well timed as 106 was preparing to return to the quarry with empties; and, with a complete absence of formalities, I took pride of place on the locomotive and soon we were chuntering and shuffling along the rickety tracks. Banana trees laden with fruit appeared on the forest's edge until the line swung into the forest itself leaving the Siantar branch behind. It was barely mid-morning yet the sun was high and the intense heat had already become oppressive. After a two-mile run the engine stopped above an enormous rope incline; this, the crew indicated, was as far as they went. Looking down I could discern the railway line continuing on through even denser forest: this second section of the line, which presumably led to the quarry, was operated by engine No. 105.

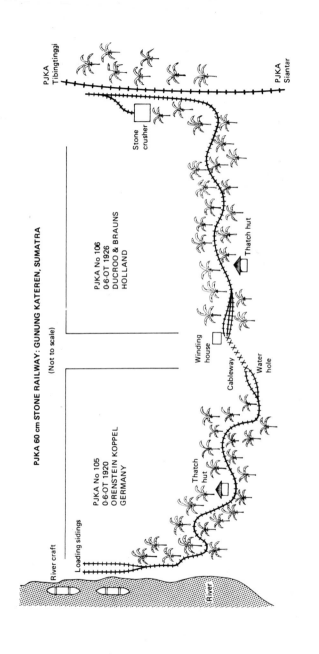

PJKA 60 cm STONE RAILWAY: GUNUNG KATEREN, SUMATRA

(Not to scale)

PJKA Tibingtinggi

PJKA Siantar

Stone crusher

PJKA No 106
0-6-OT 1926
DUCROO & BRAUNS
HOLLAND

Thatch hut

Winding house

Cableway

Water hole

PJKA No 105
0-6-OT 1920
ORENSTEIN KOPPEL
GERMANY

Thatch hut

River craft

Loading sidings

River

Anxious to find the other engine, I bade the crew farewell and, assuming it to be safe to continue – I had heard of Sumatran tigers – precariously made my descent down the long double-tracked ropeway. Reaching the bottom I was forced to rest; any untoward exertion in such heat was almost impossible. Here the forest grew denser and was ever encroaching on both sides of the track, whilst overhanging vegetation formed a green tunnel through which white heat streamed. Memories flooded back of films and stories about the tropics and now as if I were living through one of them, the jungle lay all around me.

I had been told that the quarry was within walking distance but after a mile or more the green tunnel stretched on ahead showing no sign of ending. Drenched with perspiration I developed a thirst which grew more demanding every minute – doubtless accentuated by my having had little time to adjust to tropical conditions. Fear of how to obtain drinking water was overcome when I noticed a mud-thatch hut with a fire burning outside situated in a small clearing some 25 yards distant. A woman, squatting in the entrance was engaged in baking some strange concoction and she was clearly startled both by my presence and appearance; I was later to discover that few Europeans were ever seen in the area. My mime begging for drinking water produced a doleful response, and looking very unsure she disappeared inside the hut. Was she to refuse me, or had she no water to give? Rather stupidly I stood outside fearing that she would not reappear; after more than a minute had passed I was on the point of dejectedly moving away when she re-emerged with a large pot and, gesticulating doubtfully, handed it to me. The water was very hot, almost boiling in fact, and too hot to drink. The inhabitants of the forest obtain their water from streams; thus it always has to be boiled before use: this had been done just before my arrival. Though doing little to refresh me, the hot water cured my predicament and soon I continued along the track bed with renewed vigour.

Plans to reach the quarry before engine 105 left were foiled when a high screaming whistle penetrated the forest. One hundred yards ahead an outlandish looking engine with an immense chimney appeared as, rasping, snorting and clanking the most incredible procession approached. Her comical string of four-axle waggons looked home made and seated on the stones throughout the length of the train were swarthy faced labourers looking like a band of colourful gypsies – some little more than 15 years old. The engine – essentially all chimney – chuntered past, her long rake of waggons dancing behind and the entire entourage of labourers staring incredulously.

When the train had passed, a strange thought occurred to me; the stones in those waggons were round and smooth; how could they have been quarried – yet was this not a quarry railway? Greatly intrigued I continued, the line twisted and curved its circuitous way through tangled vegetation until, after half an hour's walking, the green shrouds began to thin out and a wide river, severing the jungle in two, confronted me. Here the line ended in a little siding built on the river bank and alongside were native rafts from which stones were being unloaded.

The mystery was solved, there was no quarry; the stones being gathered from the riverbed by natives diving off rafts. This combined with the unbelievable little train I had just seen was almost too amusing for words. Two of the three men on each raft dived overboard and gleaned the stones until about two hundred had been collected – the maximum number possible without endangering the raft's safety. Upon docking, the stones were manually carried up to the waggons on wicker platters by two men, whilst the third remained on board filling the containers and placing them on the carriers' shoulders. Having given man No. One his platter, the loader then despatched man No. Two; this left him time to fill a third platter in readiness for man No. One's return: thus an efficient – if that is quite the word – operation ensued. When the

The Incredible Stone Railway

boat was finally emptied, all three men flung themselves overboard into the river to cool off. Utterly intrigued, I sat beneath
a tree watching the operation and waiting for engine 105.

It proved to be a wait of several hours and most of the
waggons had been loaded before the fussy engine's whistle
scream was heard from within the forest. My aim to relax
awhile had been thwarted by the congregation of people I had
attracted from various settlements throughout the district;
mainly children, but quite a few adults, too. Many children of
the forest had never seen a European before, perhaps not even
a picture of one, and their mesmerised preoccupation with my
pale colouring and fair hair bode a great audience.

Locomotive 105, built by the German firm of Orenstein
Koppel in 1920, was like a wild horse to ride on. Her chimney
viciously clouted the overhanging vegetation as she chugged

along sending a shower of green fragments over 'Ali Baba's forty thieves' who had re-assumed their positions along the rake. There is a growing appreciation amongst enthusiasts for light railways, but the PJKA's stone railway at Ganung Kataren is unrivalled in my experience. The locomotives, their function and environment have few parallels; the atmosphere and setting ensuring that feeling of total remove which gives birth to the refreshed spirit.

Upon returning to the rope incline it became evident that our engine was low on water and panic ensued as buckets were hastily flung out from the cab. One man, bucket in hand, dashed into the undergrowth and leapt passionately into a boggy spring where water stood two feet deep.

Incredulously, I watched a chain of labourers now juggling two buckets which, though starting full from the spring, were half empty before the man situated astride the engine could begin to fill the tank. Then, to my amazement, two empty stone waggons were actually lowered from the high level down the ropeway and no sooner had 105's tank been filled than the labourers commenced filling the waggons with water with great vigour. I then realised that the Ducroo and Brauns engine on the top section had no water supply and depended for re-supply on the waggons being hauled up from the low level. I discovered later that the bulk of the water contained in these waggons was destined for a stone-duct that had been erected along the line. Unfortunately, the waggons leaked badly and speed was of the essence in hoisting up the hapless vehicles, being promptly man handled at the incline top.

The loaded stone waggons were then hauled up one by one in exchange for empty vehicles coming down and, in anticipation of my journey back along the high level, I wearily climbed the long, steep incline – frankly, I did not trust the rope! That I was suffering from an all pervading hunger and thirst was, by now, inevitable since it was past mid-afternoon. Anticipating this, the crew of 106, after welcoming me back like a long lost brother, took me to another mud-thatch hut. I was invited to sit down on the baked earth floor whilst bananas, home made bread and lashings of warm water were duly proferred; a frugal meal, but amazingly satisfying in the circumstances. The water – none other than that carried up the ropeway – contained a large measure of mud and grit but although I could not converse with my companions, their congenial company and the cool atmosphere of the hut soon banished such incidental problems from my mind.

It was almost dark by the time I reached Siantar that evening and a violent storm was raging. Fearful bouts of thunder and lightning accompanied the deluge and Siantar's yellow dusty streets became raging torrents; the pony and trap summoned to take me up to the hotel could hardly get along. This spectacular outburst was the first of many yet to be experienced; I reached the hotel drenched.

3. 'Spirited away'

Plates 18/48/53

Just a few miles out of Jakarta lies Jatinegara – a steam depot noted for its class D52 2–8–2s. The pervading army of standardised types which has swept through the diminishing ranks of world steam has made its mark in Java with one hundred of these engines, delivered for main line working from Krupp in 1951. These relatively faceless utilitarians are of powerful and Germanic appearance – being not wholly dissimilar to the 'Reichsbahn 41' class 2–8–2s – though some engines have their modern delineation tempered by the acquisition of tenders taken from withdrawn C53 Pacifics – four-cylinder compound 'Werkspoor Greyhounds' now unfortunately out of use. An attractive blue and red plaque bearing the word 'Krupp' is attached to the D52's smokebox doors.

All D52s are oil burners and seem to smoke incessantly as

they go about their duties on the Jakarta – Surabaja main lines; most main line steam operations throughout the island now being entrusted to them. They are the PJKA's most numerous steam class and are often heard from great distances by virtue of their ghostly chime-whistles.

My initiation to the breed at Jatinegara was a sombre one since the shed, set amidst an appallingly squalid area of Jakarta's suburbs, though bursting with the D52's attributes, was also host to many homeless families who sought shelter in a variety of ingenious ways. The cabs and empty tender areas of non-active D52s were being used as dwellings complete with fitted curtains and linoleum floors; never will I forget the shock of peering into an open smokebox door to find a mother suckling a young baby, whilst lines of washing added colourful valances to the driving wheels of several engines. The potent atmosphere of steam power in an engine shed is familiar enough to enthusiasts, but few in their wildest dreams could imagine permanently living, sleeping and eating in such an environ-ment. Shower and communal bathroom was the depot water-column and as I passed this, one bather, thinking I was going to take a photograph of him, mocked me by imitating a gorilla: he leapt up and down amid the cascading water gnashing his teeth, bellowing furiously, and scratching beneath his arms. But all this was basically in good jest since that man later went to considerable effort to ascertain the times of D52 hauled trains – another instance of the innate helpfulness of the Indonesians.

A classic Javan type is the B51 4–4–0 – a type which also bears a considerable hint of German ancestry – though in this case the lineage derives from nineteenth century Prussian express passenger engines. These two-cylinder compounds are aesthetically superb: low slung boiler, elegantly tall chimney and huge dome, splashers and, on the engine's left side a low-pressure cylinder of 580 mm diameter. Over forty were built for the Dutch Colony between 1900 and 1909, principally by the German builders Hanomag and Hartmann – though a few came from Werkspoor of Amsterdam. Once an important main line class on Java's State Railway, very few actively survive today; their principal duty being the operation of passenger trains between Tanahabang in Jakarta up to Rangkasbitung – a town some 45 miles to the west.

However, a visit to the small Tanahabang shed – for all its delightful incumbents, did not produce a B51 and, as is normal in such circumstances, I attempted to elucidate information on their arrival times from Rangkasbitung – no time-table being issued! In brief, the depot foreman assured me that one would arrive at 3.00 p.m., whilst a station inspector stated the time to be 5.15. Neither were correct, no train arrived at all until 8.00 p.m. that evening and that was diesel-hauled! The following morning saw me back at Tanahabang with undiminished passion at 6.00 a.m. Enthusiastic greetings were bestowed upon me and I was told that my arrival was timely since a B51 would be coming in at 7.00 a.m. – another member of staff confirmed this with equal plausibility. Nothing arrived. In all, I had been given ten different arrival times – three agreeing with the chalked blackboard in the station entrance – but all of them were wrong. Two station officials claimed that the B51s no longer ran; others said they came in three times daily! At 10.00 a.m. a filthy diesel arrived from Rangkasbitung hauling four coaches and a waggon: this train showed signs of returning that morning and, in desperation, I decided to go with it.

Despite joining the train well before it departed, I found the coaches jammed with people; assuming the engine to be a better place on which to undertake a long journey in excessive heat, I made my way up to the front; how wrong could I be! There were seventy-five people mounted on that locomotive – a modest 3 ft 6 in. gauge secondary line diesel. Twenty-three were in the cab and the remainder situated on the front, sides and top. Undauntedly I was hauled aboard!

Upon leaving the station our train gingerly threaded its way through a maze of dwellings – colonisation of the sidings and disused rolling-stock being considerable. A few feet back from the lines lay tightly packed dwellings – a mixture of tile, thatch and wood. We passed close to line-side stalls, which but for three inches, would have collapsed – doubtless with tragic results! But this colourful scene, which stretched over a considerable distance, was, at this time, tinged with another pleasure, for as gaily and as riotously as on Monet's 'Rue Montorgueil Decked with Flags', the simple delightfully Indonesian State flag – the upper half red, the lower white – fluttered from every building, waggon and stall. It was Independence Day: August 18th. During the week of celebrations even the locomotives bear flags – special mounts for this purpose being incorporated on to smokebox-tops.

The journey was excruciatingly bad; the diesel crawled indolently along and stops were frequent: we had scarcely covered 10 miles before even the locals were beginning to look drowsy. The driver was wedged up into a far corner of the cab from which he could see little of the track ahead – presumably some agreement existed with the horde on the buffer beams that should an emergency arise, they must bang on the engine's sides. Such conditions underline part of the PJKA's malaise in that the only passengers who ever pay on a PJKA line are those unfortunate individuals who dutifully remain in the compartment or are unable to escape the ticket collector by climbing out on to the coach roof, or by obtaining a precarious place on the train by any of twenty or more hazardous methods. The engine, of course, is the driver's preserve – few ticket collectors ever infiltrating that domain. My compassion for the driver on this trip was put sharply into perspective when the hat came round. This was the driver's collection; half the price of the normal fare, no tickets issued and no questions asked; had I really thought the engine crew would suffer such discomfort for nothing? Honour among thieves was never better epitomised than by the way in which the hat finally did the round of the engine compartment and was dutifully returned to the driver full of rupiahs.

A plume of rich brown smoke erupted from a loop ahead; we were crossing with an eastbound steam train – hopefully hauled by a B51. Despite the barrage of flags I detected with surging disappointment the familiar outline of a class C27 4–6–4T. She was built to an original Swiss design of 1916 although this particular engine had been made by Sir W. G. Armstrong Whitworth, Newcastle-upon Tyne, in 1922. This engine, hauling an unbelievably well patronised six-coach Independence Day Special, rather increased my uneasy feeling that the B51s had finished. Nearly 5 hours after leaving Tanahabang the train crawled into the small town of Rangkasbitung: I was hot, jaded and suffering from claustrophobia. But the sight of two B51s steaming up in the depot yard was a great joy to behold and within seconds of leaving the train I was up at the engine shed.

It was later that afternoon that a remarkable event befell me; it was an event entirely without personal precedent and one which I am unlikely to ever forget. I had determined to travel back to Jakarta by the train which left about six o'clock – indeed the only train back – and, seeing that the train was standing in the station soon after five o'clock, it seemed a reasonable assumption that it would run. By this time one of the B51s had come into the station and stood idly in a siding: any hope that she might be taking the Jakarta train being banished since the engine was facing west. She was B5138: a Werkspoor engine of 1909 and I carried out a detailed inspection of her.

Few people could be totally insensitive to the magnetic presence of so stylish a veteran. To my amazement, I discovered that she had no steam brake – a shortage of suitable shoes having caused it to be disconnected – thus a highly dubious looking tender hand-brake was the engine's sole means of stopping. Utterly fascinated, I entered the cab; boiler pressure was well up; the engine tensely vibrating. It needed little effort to imagine her ancestors rolling majestically across the great Prussian plain hauling ornate carriages with dining cars patronised by the elegant and sophisticated; Prussian officers in their flamboyant uniforms being but one aspect of the great patriotic culture. Peering through the spectacle glasses, the green expanse of the fatherland opened up and rolled past in ever varying folds as the 'Schnellzug locomotive' plied its way towards the lights of distant Berlin. Soon the Javan crew arrived and I was jolted back to reality. Grunting an incomprehensible acknowledgement of my presence, they proceeded to back down on to a rake of decrepit rolling stock in the station. Clearly the B51s were still working passenger trains though in the opposite direction from Jakarta. With a gentle bump we coupled up and although I was anxious not to leave the cab before it was necessary, it was my firm intention to catch the train back to Jakarta – all my belongings being in my hotel there. Suddenly the engine moved forward, at first I assumed this to be a station movement but within seconds I realised that a journey had begun and that, under partial mesmerisation, I was being 'spirited away'.

I had no idea where we were going and although the crew were friendly enough, the language barrier made communication impossible. The epic way in which B5138 stormed out of Rangkasbitung that evening did justice to her Prussian lineage as, with trilling whistle, she charged through the suburbs and out of the town – the State flags fluttering either side of her chimney. Any ideas of my getting off swiftly at the first station were soon banished; the likelihood of my getting back to Rangkasbitung that night seemed remote. My maps were all in the Jakarta hotel and I could make no assessment of the locale; better though to stay with the engine – a decision I was not to regret.

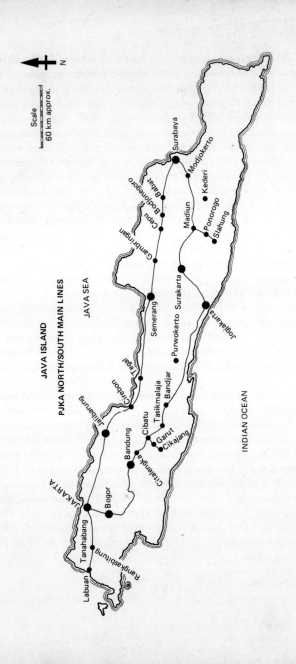

JAVA ISLAND

PJKA NORTH/SOUTH MAIN LINES

JAVA SEA

INDIAN OCEAN

Scale
60 km approx.

N

JAKARTA

Labuan
Tanahabang
Rangkasbitung
Bogor
Bandung
Citalengka
Cikajang
Garut
Cibatu
Tasikmalaja
Bandjar
Purwokerto
Cirebon
Bumiajen
Tegal
Semarang
Gambringan
Cepu
Bodjonegoro
Batat
Surabaya
Modjokerto
Kederi
Ponorogo
Slahung
Madiun
Surakarta
Joglakarta

The B51 burned a mixture of coal, wood and oil but during the journey's early stages the fireman was principally using coal. Dusk was rapidly advancing and soon our engine was pumping black exhaust into an azure sky; a pungently smelling frothy smoke continually sweeping around the cab and down the train. Our speed was greater than I had imagined possible, the engine, like an anguished beast, ferociously headed through the darkening landscape. The 'rollicking plink' of side rods had a musical clarity the equal of which I had not heard since the old Midland Railway 4-4-0 'Simples' were eased round the curved junction at Wigston North on the Midland main line. The veteran's violent lurching over the rough track beds was stimulating enough; her pounding intensity seldom letting up; though on the few occasions when she was eased, a most delightful aroma of coal smoke wafted back through the fire-hole doors and into the cab; this, when combined with the sweet clinging smell of oil produced a glorious sensation.

Darkness had fallen by the time we reached the first station – a wayside halt which only merited our presence for a matter of seconds. Soon the drama returned in all its affray, a hiss of steam escaping from the front end became audible and made an exciting foil to the throbbing rasps of exhaust. Speed mounted terrifyingly and the engine became a mass of churning pulsating machinery: the whistle screamed and wailed in long eerie bursts as we sped past lonely villages and small un-gated crossings, but remote as we were and dark as it was, a few ox-carts could invariably be discerned momentarily lit up by the swirling incandesence of B5138's fire.

Without warning she hit a downgrade and the engine was really opened out; the roar became hypnotic. It was impossible to estimate our speed, the darkness outside revealed nothing from which a bearing might be taken; the crew, bathed in a shimmering orange glow, clung tenaciously to the cabsides. The fire, white hot, lit up the black exhaust trail which raced in a swirling slipstream above the cab roof. We could to all intents and purposes have been hitting a hundred miles per hour! Those hypnotic rhythms of escaping steam, exhaust, and spinning rods, combined with the smell of oil smoke and steam, which oozed from that engine, along with the thundering intensity with which it hurtled itself through the blackness – swathed in golden fire – can only be described as orgastic. I had come to Indonesia to find the dinosaur and by perfect fortune had found one in full cry; the last of her breed; a Prussian phantom; and a living ghost of the great nineteenth century steam age.

With many miles now behind us it seemed that the country was beginning to flatten out and over the rice-paddies fire-flies could be seen; little points of light which in places were so dense as to merge into fiery clusters of light. It was about this time that our coal supply ran out and the logs, which had hitherto been ignored, came into their own. The B51 responded with a flurry of sparks, brilliantly cascading in the paths of the fire-flies; the darkness bursting into a brightly illuminated tapestry; surging trajectories, darting spirals and pin-points of silver and orange light forming ever-changing patterns in the star-lit sky. Suddenly as the train sped onwards through different terrain, the fire-flies were left behind, and like the eclipse of a fireworks display observed with the awe of child-hood – the magic was gone.

We slowed down as we approached another station; would this be our destination? No, it was but another dismal little halt sullenly lit by oil-lamps. Several mysterious figures carrying sacks and boxes left the gloomy interior of the train and disappeared from view. Windows on Indonesian branch line stock are usually either jammed tightly in the open or shut positions; they do not possess electric light, the method of illumination usually being candles; alternate compartments in our six-coach train being thus equipped.

A whistle was heard in the gloom and steam squirted from the cylinders as, with throaty coughs, our compound slid forwards into the darkness. Within another 15 minutes the engine slowed down again and speckled lights could be seen ahead; this I rightly concluded was our destination. The town was Labuan – which I was later to discover is located on the west coast of Java. The engine was to remain here overnight, returning at 5 a.m. the following morning and the crew, realising my predicament ordered a betjak to lead me to some accommodation. I bade the crew farewell promising to rejoin them next morning. Independence celebrations were in full swing in Labuan: bands played, fireworks exploded in the night sky, processions thronged the streets; but I was too exhausted to share in the excitement. Fifteen hours had elapsed since my arrival in Tanahabang; the intense heat, fatigue and lack of food had made their mark.

My nocturnal refuge turned out to be a low slung wooden house on the outskirts of the town and, to my relief, the proprietor spoke English. While a welcome meal was being prepared by his family, he explained that Labuan was a quiet but beautiful place; immediately behind the house lay a wonderful coral beach – not a hundred yards away he emphasised! He entreated me to stay for a few days and enjoy the Javan coast but I explained that my visit came as much of a surprise to me as it had done to him, and that furthermore I was anxious to retrieve my belongings from the hotel in Jakarta.

Though greatly revived by an excellently prepared meal, I still felt unequipped mentally to answer the stream of questions posed by the family as to my mission in the town. I tried to explain the story of the B51 and the strange circumstances of my journey. They listened with great interest as my narrative was translated to them word for word by my host. Altogether there were ten people in the family. It was, however, relaxing to speak English once again and it was well after midnight before we all retired; a call having been arranged for me at 4.15 a.m. so that I should be at the station before 5.00.

The distressing combination of over-exhaustion and belligerent mosquitoes in my room effectively banished any hope of real sleep, but even so I must have dozed off and was not aroused until 5.00 when a servant woke me. Realising my plight, I dashed out of the house and ran through the empty streets towards the town centre hoping that the train might still be in the station, but when I heard a familiar exhaust beat and whistle call echo over the silent dwelling places, I knew that B5138 was on her way. Cursing and feeling acutely sorry for myself, I halted awhile, wondering what on earth to do. The inhabitants of Labuan were sleeping off the effects of the previous evening's celebrations, and so I made my way through the still deserted streets to the beach, the early morning sun already heralding another day of intense heat.

Since the next train was not due until afternoon – assuming that it ran at all – I was persuaded to catch a bus 'direct' to Jakarta: my informant omitting to tell me that the trip included a round tour of Java. The bus, of incredible decrepitude, hurtled along flat out scattering all and sundry from its path. It was a harrowing and hair-raising journey, the sum total of minor incidents en route being: two punctures; overheated engine; loss of entire cargo of rice from roof; and a dangerous skid which promised to terminate in a stagnant pond. Fatalities were three squashed chickens and possibly a dog which leapt out of the bus into thick undergrowth. It would be an economy in effort if the Indonesian bus drivers were to leave their hooters permanently on full blast and simply switch them off when not needed. I arrived in Jakarta 7 hours after leaving Labuan. How I regretted missing the B51!

4. The Mallets' Last Stronghold

The Mallet types ultimate flowering gave the world the biggest steam giants it will ever see – the Union Pacific Railroads 4–8–8–4 'Big Boys' each weighing 520 tons. This 'Brontosaurus' of steam bellowed over the great American plains in much the same way as the dinosaur did until it too succumbed to the onslaught of a succeeding 'order'. Indeed the Mallet story itself is one of ingenious evolutionary development since it was as long ago as 1884 when a Frenchman, Anatole Mallet, devised a small semi-articulated tank engine in which the main frames were split into two units; the rear one rigid, the front one articulated. However, Mallet's principal interest lay in compounding and he provided his engine with four cylinders; two high-pressure ones driving the rear unit, and two low-pressure ones operating the articulated one.

The Mallet evolved in compound form as specified by its originator, but it was primarily heralded as an articulated locomotive and, on account of its weight being widely spread, it was swiftly adopted for use over sharply curved routes with lightly laid track. Mallet's initial engine – a 60 cm 0–4–4–0T was the precursor of many similar industrial designs for narrow gauge networks and it is especially interesting that Sumatra's palm-oil plantations are prolific users of the 0–4–4–0T Mallet previously mentioned in the book.

However, the Mallet engine's development acquired a different and more dynamic aspect when, after graduating through a succession of main line tank types, it emerged as a fully-fledged tender engine for main line use – Hungary being a notable early recipient. But the emergent Mallet was destined to colonise the New World and first appeared there in 1904 when the Baltimore and Ohio Railroad acquired an 0–6–6–0. Over the next 40 years, 3,500 Mallet engines were to see service in America; some, like the 1904 engine, being of unprecedented proportions. Certain Mallets, including many latter day American ones, were characterised by a shift away from compounding, though the classic example is traditionally regarded as a four-cylinder compound.

Soon after its rapid disappearance from North America the main line Mallet tender engine became rare; some authorities regarding it to be obsolete: in contrast its articulated relative – the Garratt – was active in many countries. This state of affairs existed until the discovery of the Javan engines when, in a mountainous part of the island, appropriately studded with extinct volcanoes, a colony of Mallets was unearthed containing giant 2–8–8–0 Compounds – direct descendants of an original Alco class – and some slightly smaller 2–6–6–0. Compounds from European builders. Also, for good measure, were some ancient 2–6–6–0 Compound tanks of no mean proportions.

The Javan Mallet story began at a time when the type was in great vogue in America. Although very few American engines saw service in the Dutch East Indies, there was seen to be a case for the State Railway acquiring some big Mallet thoroughbreds for operating Java's difficult routes, especially the mountainous section of the Jakarta – Surabaja main line between Bandung and Tasikmalaja. In 1916, the first eight 2–8–8–0's were delivered, and classified DD50, followed three years later by a dozen engines known as DD51's: all were direct from Alco. The DD50's, are now believed to be completely non-existent and although no DD51's remain active, a number of derelict examples can be found as evidenced by Plate 33. The active giants are the DD52's – to all intents and purposes identical with the American machines but from European builders. Ten were built; three from Hanomag and four from Werkspoor in 1923, followed by three from Hartmann (1924). This total of thirty 2–8–8–0 Mallets was matched a few years later by an equal number of slightly smaller 2–6–6–0s, classified CC50. These were simply a scaled down variant of their larger relations and all emanated from Europe – in this case SLM Switzerland and Werkspoor Holland. Built over the years 1927/8, the CC50's were intended for secondary main line services as well as branch line duties.

However, Mallet tank engines had been in service on the State system since just before the turn of the century when, in 1899 the first BB10 0–4–4–2T arrived from Hartmann. Although a few isolated examples of this older class still survive, the main tank class saw service in 1904, when the larger CC10 2–6–6–0T first arrived from the same builder. Deliveries continued up to 1911 by which time thirty-four examples had been put into traffic; some later engines coming from Schwartzkopf and Werkspoor. These, in common with the BB10s, are branch line engines and a number survive active today.

The world famous Mallet centre is at Cibatu – a small junction on the Jakarta – Surabaya main line from which trains head southwards along a branch to Garut and Cikajang. Here with the big tender types working main line 'mixeds' eastwards to Tasikmalaja and west to Citjalengka and CC10's, along with the odd CC50, on the Cikajang branch, is the depot with a 100 per cent. Mallet allocation; comprised of three different classes. The main line sees the giants slogging over 1 in 40 grades against a stark volcanic backdrop with the line traversing high, open-sided viaducts spanning awesome ravines with sheer drops measuring hundreds of feet. On either side of the Mallet's domain the Krupp D52's reign supreme on such steam services as remain.

Unfortunately it is a hard battle to keep the big Mallets running and although they are responsible for working mixed trains over a considerable section of main line, mechanical failures have not infrequently caused them to lie dormant, with all trains – other than the through diesel-hauled expresses – being cancelled. Such a situation dominated my visit to Cibatu when, after months of eager anticipation, I arrived to discover that the DD52's – three on the active roster – had not turned a wheel for eight weeks. Bits of them lay all around the depot and an ardent team of fitters, supervised by a permanently harassed depot foreman, were unable, with the economic circumstances besetting them, to get the giants working with any degree of reliability. So my dream of seeing them active amongst the majestic volcanic mountains and valleys was not to transpire. Only the Cikajang branch, was in operation on account of a complete lack of alternative mainline motive-power – the D52's not being suitable as they have a tendency to spread the track when working hard.

It was a woeful shedmaster who explained the circumstances, but he offered some cheer by saying that CC5017 would be working between Cibatu and Garut the following day and that a good time to see her leave would be on the 9.00 a.m. departure. Making my base in a nearby hotel, I took full advantage of the health-giving spring water which flowed, naturally warm, to the hotel from inside an adjacent volcano. The water, flowing through ducts, traversed the entire building and was a marvellous relief in a land not noted for sophisticated plumbing. The balmy and invigorating water offered some recompense for the bitter disappointment of that afternoon and, after a predictable menu of chicken and rice, I further dowsed my sorrows in lashings of 'Indomilk' and bananas.

During the early hours of the following morning, I awoke suddenly in pitch darkness with a conviction that the bed was rolling across the floor. Apart from my being alone in the room, the bed was not on castors so I doubted the plausibility of my conclusion – especially since there was no accompanying sound; yet, unless I were dreaming, my bed was not only moving but also at an ever increasing pace. Someone must be pushing it, I concluded, and intending to catch the culprit, I jumped out of bed and put on the light. The room was empty and the bed in its correct place. That I had been dreaming was the only possible conclusion, especially as the phenomenon had now disappeared completely.

Pondering over the incident next morning, there seemed no likely solution to the mystery and it was still at the back of my mind when I arrived at Cibatu depot. Within five minutes the shedmaster confronted me with two meaningful facts; firstly, he asked me if I had felt the earth movements during the night – he explained that the terrestrial disturbance, which came from an adjacent volcano, only occurred about once per year: secondly, CC5017 had failed – she was in the shed surrounded by a swarm of fitters. What was to happen over the following 48 hours not only underlined the current status of PJKA steam power but also reveals some of the inherent difficulties involved in tracking down historic steam locomotives.

The Cikajang branch calls for two locomotives, usually CC10s, but as No. CC1030 – one of the engines, had been undergoing repairs for some days, the Mallet tender had taken its place. However, now this had succumbed, only No. CC1007 remained on the line. She was the only active engine at Cibatu. Accordingly No. CC1007 which had been assigned to the Garut–Cikajang section and had come in that morning piloting CC5017 on the 6.36 ex Garut for servicing, took over the Cibatu–Garut trains; apart from this being the most important section, the next Garut–Cikajang train was not due until 14.10 and, it was fervently hoped, the fitters might just coax No. CC1030 into action for this – she had already been lit up! The table on the following page will clarify.

The second locomotive, which on this particular morning was CC1007, having arrived at Garut from Cikajang piloted the first locomotive up to Cibatu for servicing then, still piloting, returned on the 12.30 in readiness for the 14.10 departure from Garut. The double-heading occurs providing both engines are either CC10s or a CC10 and CC50 – as on this particular day. Should both engines happen to be CC50s, then the second one runs light as the combined weight of two heavy engines would damage the bridges.

Having seen No. CC1007 make its belated departure to

MALLET SERVICE
CIBATU – GARUT – CIKAJANG
SCHEDULED TIMES AS AT SEPTEMBER 1974

(1st Locomotive)

Cibatu – Garut		Garut – Cibatu	
05.00	06.10	06.36	07.46
09.00	10.10	10.51	11.59
12.30	13.40	14.36	15.46
16.35	17.45	18.36	19.46

(2nd Locomotive)

Garut – Cikajang	
14.10	15.49

(loco. remains overnight
at Cikajang)

06.14	04.35

Garut at 9.50, there seemed little point in my remaining at Cibatu and I returned to my hotel situated near Garut.

At 13.30, I turned up at Garut Station to see the double-header arrive and to travel with No. CC1030 down to Cikajang. But in the station entrance a large blackboard protruded above a sea of motley humanity blazoning the pronouncement '14.10 to Cikajang cancelled' – the fact that the stock, jammed from end to end with people, was standing in the station seemed little to do with anything. Evidently No. CC1030 could not be repaired in time and I presumed No. CC1007 would continue on the Cibatu–Garut section. This was not to be – it is fatal to assume anything in Indonesia – since the train eventually turned up at 15.05 behind none other than CC1030; she immediately ran round her train and prepared to return to Cibatu: thus, in the interim, No.CC1007 had failed and No.CC1030 had taken her place. Within minutes of arriving, the Cibatu stock was full and this provided the remarkable sight of two packed trains facing in opposite directions and only one steamable engine within 50 miles; needless to say, no one looked the least bit surprised or even concerned! However, all was not lost, No.CC1007's indisposition was allegedly temporary and she would be double-heading down on the 16.35 from Cibatu, after which she could proceed to Cikajang. This joyous fact, having been well announced by the station 'criers', meant that the incumbents of the Cikajang stock faced a wait of several hours and those who had not long since fallen asleep, promptly proceeded to do so.

My reappearance at the station at 17.45 to see the two CC10s arrive found no change in the situation – apart from a vast increase in would-be travellers. I had expected the train to be late on account of its delayed departure that afternoon, but even I was surprised when it did not arrive until 19.30. To my utmost delight the train arrived, not behind the two CC10s but with No.CC5017 piloting No.CC1030. Eight cylinders hauling three diminutive coaches – incredible! Evidently they had not got CC1007 working after all, but had persuaded CC5017 to work again – when the looming front end of the big Mallet appeared in the station lights I was very thrilled indeed. It was now decided that the CC50 would work the Cibatu section and CC1030 would go south to Cikajang; thus after a five hour wait the Mallet coupled up to the Cikajang stock whilst the tender engine prepared to return to Cibatu with the late running 18.35 – Plate 12 being made during the changeover.

With most travellers asleep in the coaches and vans, No. CC1030, leaking profusely from all cylinders, shuffled away into the darkness with great aplomb and a lovely macabre wailing of her whistle. Next, the big Mallet – like a sledgehammer to a walnut – coupled up to her three diminutive four-wheel coaches and with a heavy masculine whistle chime – which not only rivalled the very best of American traditions but furthermore made her sound as if she were at the head of a 3,000-ton load – slipped away effortlessly with hardly a rasp from her chimney. It had been a fine moment; here in this small branch line station had been two mainline Mallets, both tender and tank varieties, and standing side by side boiling up.

The table indicates an allowed time between Garut and Cikajang of 1 hr 39 mins but because of the CC10's ailing condition, they were regularly taking 2½ hours since this extremely scenic section has gradients of 1 in 25. Although I was up at Cibatu the following morning by 7.45 a.m. to see the double-header arriving, I knew that they would be late since the trains connected at Garut. Sitting by the trackside near Cibatu I waited, but as time went on, I felt instinctively that something was wrong. Eventually from some miles away CC5017's chime whistle rang out – at last they were coming; it was just after 10.00! As the train approached I saw that CC5017 was in front – surely she was train engine: CC1030 ought to be leading! As they passed I noticed that the tender Mallet was hauling an inanimate looking CC1030, then to my utter chagrin I saw the set of motion of the leading tank was damaged and partially dismantled – she was dead! She had dropped her motion when coming up from Cikajang that morning and thus CC5017 had entered the section to haul her back – after a taxi load of fitters had left Cibatu at 5.30 to locate the stranded Mallet and taken down the motion before she could be moved! Apparently the engine had failed half way round a hillside and was inaccessible by road – the fitters having had to embark upon a fairly lengthy cross-country trek; the unhappy engine's dismembered pieces of valve gear were heaped up on the cab floor!

Truly out for the count, CC1030 was pushed into the engine shed where she joined her equally unfortunate sister; CC5017 now assumed sole command. Since it was decreed that neither CC10 could readily be made to work again the Garut–Cikajang section was shut until further notice. Although it was now after 11.00, CC5017 still had to wait before returning to Garut with the delayed 9.00 as the connecting express from

Bandjar–Jakarta was running nearly three hours late. The other connecting train from Jakarta, was running so late that it could be disregarded – it was generally felt at Cibatu that the Mallet would be back from Garut before it arrived! Finally the Mallet got away soon after 12.00.

I remained at Cibatu that afternoon. When by 5 p.m. – long after the Jakarta train had arrived – CC5017 had not returned, I developed a familiar feeling of consternation. Many people were on the station, some from the Jakarta train but many others had congregated for the 4.35. On my way to the traffic office I met the station master's assistant ruefully carrying a large blackboard – it read; 'Garut trains cancelled owing to engine failure'. Thus No.CC5017 had succumbed and the famous all Mallet depot was temporarily silenced; all trains were cancelled until further notice – a Javan tragedy indeed!

5. Night-time at Purwokerto

Having abandoned the Mallet country, I moved eastwards into central Java and eventually arrived in Purwokerto; a junction with a magnificent allocation of locomotives. It was late evening and my hastily secured accommodation, though close to the railway, was far from salubrious.

In lieu of running water the washroom contained a large water tank as well as a dunking pan – in this case a battered one gallon, 'Glo-Tex' paint tin. Armed with the pan, but lacking soap, mirror or towel, I endeavoured to remove some degree of the day's dust. The washroom's sole means of illumination was a candle; this flickered and spat precariously and twice during the washing operation, I put it out altogether and, in the process of trying to relight it, dropped my matches in the watertank. Being without light meant that the cockroaches – nicknamed Abdillah's – could not be seen; imagination running riot as to where they might be. My consternation was unrelieved when I discovered fish in the watertank – five goldfish merrily swimming around! But this was Indonesia where everything is larger than life; a country as exciting as any in the world: so, feeling refreshed at least and ignoring the late hour, I set off from my spartan abode for the adjacent engine sheds where many more things, larger than life, were to be found.

After crossing the darkened track, the line-up of fascinating beasts which protruded through the gloom almost defy description; it was as if one were walking into an exotic dream. First came two B51 4–4–0s sadly derelict with wheels missing and some of their ornate boiler mountings removed. Yet their majesty remained undiminished. Immediately behind them was a B52 0–4–0 tender engine – surely one of the most veritable gems left anywhere today; the clockwork train engine come true. These 'Hornbys', as they are nicknamed, are employed on roadside tramways and very lightly laid branches. They number twenty-seven engines all delivered from Hartmann between 1908/13 for the Semarang Cheribon Steamtram Co. (SCS) – a private line which built a supplementary railway network to the State system.

On an adjacent road and very much in steam was a B22 'Skirt Tank' – a two-cylinder compound 0–4–2 with tanks, looking like valances, placed over the driving wheels. The B22s, again from Hartmann, numbered twenty engines delivered to the Nederlandse Indische Spoorweg (NIS), between 1898/1900. Most still exist though one engine, in South Sumatra, has had its tanks removed and been coupled to a four-wheeled tender from a scrapped B50 2–4–0 (Sharp Stewart 1880). Other 'Skirt Tanks' of the 0–6–0 type exist in rural use, being similar but larger than a B22: all were built for the NIS system. The combination of Skirt Tanks, Hornbys and a plethora of 0–4–0 Tram Engines provides Java with a remarkable set of diminutive engines for cross-country work.

Particularly noteworthy amongst such lines is the Surabaja Steam Tram – usually comprised of nineteenth century Beyer Peacock 0–4–0 Tram Engine hauling two ancient coaches – which runs through the city and into the docks, incurring en route the most unbelievable chaos. Not infrequently does this fantastic little train turn down one-way streets in error; not infrequently is it held up, squealing furiously, because a road vehicle has been parked across its track; and not infrequently is it reduced to walking pace as it attempts to clear a path through the thronged city streets. Once, when all the Tram Engines failed, services were temporarily suspended and within a week a large market, complete with stalls and stock-piles, had been built over the track. Later when the train ran again it was confronted by this obstacle and, as the little engine stood whistling and snorting, the entire market had to be dismantled – an operation which took 3 hours!

In absolute contrast with the B22 loomed the gigantic form of a CC50 Mallet standing in the depot entrance with steam pouring from its safety valves. She towered high above the smaller engines – her tender alone being sufficient to dwarf them. Another engine could be heard in steam behind the Mallet and there, as if an articulated giant were not enough, stood a rigid 'Centipede' – an enormous 2–12–2 Well-Tank engine classified F10. No less than twenty-eight of these magnificent brutes were put into service and they perform over hilly routes in both Java and Sumatra.

Entering the shed building, to the incredulous but welcoming gaze of the night foreman, several C28 4–6–4Ts were discovered. These 'colonial-looking' passenger tanks are of a highly imposing appearance, their enormous windshields merging into long side tanks, giving them a sleek express-passenger styling. Indeed many fast services involving speeds in excess of 70 m.p.h. were once undertaken by them. An enlargement of the earlier C27 4–6–4Ts, the 80-ton C28s were all built in Germany during 1921 and were a typical product of that era. They are said to be the most popular steam engines on the PJKA – fifty-eight were built, all remaining in existence today. Immediately behind the C28s came a real veteran – a C11 2–6–0T with her huge chimney and dome well laced with copper and brass: what a contrast she made having been built to a design first prepared in 1879! These delicious antiquities – the PJKA's oldest engines – are usually high on the priority list of rail enthusiasts who visit Java.

Now confronting me was the gleaming copper and brass of an immaculate C54 Class 4–6–0 – this class, along with some close relations of classes C51/2, provide an important link in the progression of Javan express passenger types from the 2–4–0 up to the Pacific – Java being able to produce examples of all types with the exception of an Atlantic. The handsome engine standing before me was one of a class built for the SCS in 1922. In their heyday, the C54s once operated expresses between Semerang and Cheribon – part of what is now the north coast route between Jakarta and Surabaja.

After the 4–6–0 came another Mallet: behind this lay yet another rare treat – a D51 2–8–2 – again in resplendent condition. The D51s are especially interesting since all ten were originally built by Hartmann in 1920 for the Hedjaz Railway, but after Lawrence of Arabia blew up that line the engines were eventually diverted to Java where a handful survive today on secondary duties; the Purwokerto engines working to Propuk.

Finding myself back in the shed yard I totted up a total of sixteen engines on shed comprising nine totally different classes ranging from diminutive roadside 0–4–0s up to big American-style 2–6–6–0 Mallets with nineteenth century 2–6–0Ts, Prussian 4–4–0s, 4–6–0s, Hedjaz 2–8–2s, express tank engines and 2–12–2 Well-Tanks in between! There can be few steam depots in the world today capable of producing such an assortment.

It will be seen that the PJKA classification system uses an initial letter in alphabetical sequence to indicate the number of coupled wheels, i.e. B – four coupled: C – six coupled etc. This is followed by a class number of two figures; the numbers below fifty representing tank/tram classes, the ones above – tender engines. After the letter and class number comes the individual engine number, thus F1002 is a ten coupled tank engine, number two in the class sequence. Exactly the same principle applies with the Mallets, except that the initial letter is doubled in accordance with the two sets of coupled wheels – CC1007 being a 2–6–6–0 Mallet, tank-engine number seven and DD5208 being a 2–8–8–0 Mallet tender-engine number eight. The ex Deli Railway engines in Northern Sumatra, though now a part of PJKA stock, retain their original classification.

Since most of the engines encountered at Purwokerto were quite new to me I spent over two hours in the depot and it was well after midnight before I made my way back to the hotel. As I left the depot yard the 'Skirt Tank' suddenly wheezed into life and began trundling around with curls of fire wafting from her chimney; like most engines present, she was dependent upon wood for fuel.

6. The Pallid Phantoms of Jogjakarta

Plates 10/30

Jogjarkarta lies under Mount Merapi, a smoking volcano in central Java. In this ancient city the plodding world of ox-drawn carts gives way to the chromium-plated modernity of a new era; here the kampongs and rice-paddies recede under the encroaching forms of a universal architecture; this affords little harmony with either the island's general environment or the cultural remains of civilisations past for which Jogjakarta is so famous. It seems appropriate that this thriving university town should hold the diesel works and training centre of the PJKA.

However, the air of modernity at Balakarga Works is severely tempered by the rows of diesels lying awaiting attention in weed choked sidings. The majority need spares, which under prevailing circumstances, are unobtainable though others have either seized up, burnt up or been partially wrecked. They present a dismal picture in a country desperately striving to improve its economy. Little short of one hundred of them lie awaiting attention and one muses that should they ever be returned to traffic – and kept there – it would have a severely detrimental effect on the future of PJKA steam.

The works yard covers a considerable area and some of its periphery is extensively overgrown. At first sight, no steam engines are apparent anywhere within the works confines, but having diligently searched the far corners and forged my way through much undergrowth, I discovered what I had been searching for; the last priceless remnants of an early evolutionary form – the 0–4–2 tender express-engine. Though reduced to a blaze of rust and partially obscured by tropical fronds, the British delineation of the four standard gauge (4 ft 8½ in.) 0–4–2s with large diameter coupled wheels was unmistakeable. They had been shipped out by Beyer Peacock of Manchester from the early 1880's onwards, though judging by their styling, the design could easily be dated back to 1870. They had not turned a wheel in over 30 years, certainly not since the Japanese invaded Java in 1942 and shipped away all standard gauge equipment – an action which left the island with a uniform 3 ft 6 in. gauge network.

The engines were relics of the old Dutch NIS, a company involved in the piecemeal construction of the south main line from Jakarta–Surabaja, which operated a 4 ft 8½ in. section between Jogjakarta and Surakarta – although from 1899 onwards, a third rail was added to facilitate through running of 3 ft 6 in. gauge trains. The NIS had completed a 4 ft 8½ in. gauge line from Semarang–Gundih–Surakarta–Jogjakarta in 1872; this latter section being later used as part of the through main line.

Whether these 0–4–2s were follow-up engines of an original 1872 type ordered from Beyer Peacock's for the NIS, or were simply a later design prepared from 1880 onwards is not known, though I suspect the former. Although not used since the Japanese invasion in 1942 they could, of course, have been derelict prior to that date; this might explain why they were not exported away to Manchuria. Thus, in absolute speculation they could have been derelict for nearer 50 years! What is known with reasonable certainty, is that these engines represent the last existing remnants, not only of Java's standard gauge network, but more important of the classic 0–4–2 express engine itself. Amongst other engines with them was a Beyer Peacock outside framed 0–6–0 goods engine of 1885 and this gem bore more than a hint of Kirtley's numerous outside framed 0–6–0s of the Midland Railway produced between 1863/74 – a type of engine which survived in Britain until 1951.

The 0–4–2, along with its more prolific relative the 2–4–0, evolved in Britain during the 1830's. Perhaps the most famous is 'Lion' built in 1838 for the Liverpool and Manchester Railway. After little over 20 years service, 'Lion' found herself dumped in a siding at Liverpool Dock as a stationary engine to drive pumping machinery. She was destined to lie in that siding for nearly 70 years until being rescued and restored to her original condition under the auspices of Henry Fowler – Chief Mechanical Engineer of the LMS. This epic 0–4–2 has since become world famous for her part in the film, 'Titfield Thunderbolt'. Australia's first steam engines were 0–4–2s shipped from Britain in the 1850's – the Javanese relics bearing a superficial resemblance to them, but in 1882 the type reached its zenith with Stroudley's yellow livered 'Gladstones' for the London Brighton and South Coast Railway.

For many years now, the 0-4-2 has been regarded as extinct and the discovery of these Beyer Peacocks, albeit as ghosts, is as heartening as it is exciting. The two plates depict a feeling of the grotesque so characteristic of old derelict engines and No.30 is made in deference to Java's numerous thunderstorms; the rain providing the rust and vegetation; the lightning serving to intensify the engine's awesome appearance.

7. Madiun Works

Plates 9/33

Locomotive works hold a fascination of their own; they are, like the big running sheds, important focal points of a system, yet their atmosphere is totally different. They are places where one can get closest of all to the steam engine's illusive personality, for although little action is to be found, the great jigsaw of parts serves to make the whole more vivid. In Picasso's early cubist paintings, fragmented form was similarly placed in such a way as to intensify one's experience of the real object. Few workshops can be more rewarding than Madiun; the PJKA's steam centre in East Java. Quite apart from the long straggling buildings – which look as if they would be more at home in a rain-swept Lancashire setting than in tropical Java – the works has many magical ingredients – a tremendous variety of different classes are present; engines in all stages of overhaul – with an impressive line-up awaiting shops; ex works engines fully painted; and, last but not least, a scrap line.

Although Madiun is the only steam works in Java, much of the machinery is old fashioned and the total work force numbers but eight-hundred. Many more works are needed, but the money is not available – some 40 per cent of the country's working population is permanently unemployed – and, on average, only one locomotive can be outshopped per week.

With an estimated 30 per cent of its diesel fleet inactive at Jogjakarta, the island inevitably places a great dependence upon its array of vintage steam engines, but the ravages of age and neglect have left these in little better condition. Indonesia has no iron foundry, thus spares – even tubes – have to be specially ordered from abroad, notably Japan. This in itself is bad enough, but the PJKA have no less than fifty-two types of steam locomotive on their books for Java alone: the cost and complexity of keeping such a fleet running would be bad enough in the developed and industrialised countries, but out in Java it has now assumed nightmare proportions.

The diverse range of engines from the old companies of pre-nationalisation days is greatly apparent. Little attempt at standardisation has been carried out but there is one exception – the 100 Krupp mixed-traffic D52 2–8–2s of 1951. Since these now form a mainstay of power, the works does attempt to out-shop an engine within eight months of arrival; the time for other classes usually being well over a year. Partially due to poor maintenance, the D52s are not noted for high mileages between shopping, about fifteen permanently being in Madiun: boiler corrosion is said to be a particular fault with these engines. Excessive cannibalisation is one way to keep some vestige of the fleet in operation and engines of many classes, though allegedly awaiting shops, have since become remarkably naked in appearance. Most engines should have brake-shoes, but as these are particularly difficult to obtain, it has become policy to remove the steam-brake altogether. The shopping rate is but one aspect of a wider operational problem since a freshly overhauled engine, might upon its return to the home depot, be promptly stopped on account of fuel shortage; whereas another depot with adequate fuel supplies might be eagerly awaiting return of an engine from the works. It is diffi-cult to correlate these two problems at the erecting shop level because apart from shopping being such a lengthy process, the fuel situation is an ever changing one. Shortage of wood is a major problem and Madiun have a policy of slowly converting the steam fleet to oil burning. Coal is mined in neighbouring Sumatra but its shipment and distribution to locomotive depots is an immense and costly operation beyond the country's means.

Conversely, as PJKA readily appreciate, such a position constitutes a paradise to the steam lover for this authority maintains the last great 'pre-grouping' conglomeration in the world. No sooner had I entered the works than one engine was seen to be racing up and down puffing away with full regulator and whistle blowing between the lines of silent engines. Upon finally emerging it proved to be a C11 2–6–0T painted in resplendent black with an enormous brass dome gleaming in the strong sunlight. She had rounded cylinders, a high flared chimney and massive tool box mounted on the tank. Radiantly ex-shops, she was a veritable stalwart having been built in 1879.

This fussy little tank-engine made a welcome comparison with the long line of fifty engines awaiting shops – a pathetic total considering the output rate. Notable in the line-up were CC50/DD52 Mallets, 2–4–0T/2–6–0T of 1880's origin, two classes of 4–4–0 express types and Tram Engines – along with numerous incidental tank classes. One particular veteran was B5001 – the first Sharp Stewart 2–4–0 of 1880 – a class still carrying their original boiler shells. Apparently Madiun is no longer overhauling the big DD52 Mallets and I wonder, thinking back to my experiences at Cibatu if, in fact, these might now be finished; certainly the one needing to go to Madiun will be consigned to the dump and never outshopped. In all, over twenty different types were waiting works. The erecting shop contained examples of six classes: B52 0–4–0, C12–6–0T, C27/28 4–6–4Ts, D52 2–8–2 and a CC10 2–6–6–0T Mallet.

But possibly the most dramatic aspect of those works was the scrap line where engines lay rotting their way back into the

Workplate of PJKA Mallet DD5205

earth. If the PJKA paid for them to be cut up, the scrap would have to be exported to a nearby developed nation; it simply is not worth it – better to leave them. The rusted giants decaying amongst the dense vegetation made an incredible spectacle; here, the poignancy of old age came into its own every bit as much as if the engines were out steaming on the track. The partially dismembered form of a B13 2–4–0T fenced in by young guava trees set the mood for many other similar hulks but I will never forget the heart surging delight experienced when I discovered a C53 'Werkspoor Pacific' – one of a beautiful breed of twenty, four-cylinder compound Pacifics shipped out by the Dutch firm between 1917/22. Gone are the days when these sleek thoroughbreds used to race the length of the island with expresses between Jakarta and Surabaja; all are now out of use, but their greyhound-like appearance leaves no doubt as to their original purpose: it was little short of tantalising to imagine one of these engines at the head of a long express speeding in the 'seventies' and spinning its 1,600 mm driving wheels across the Javan landscape. The plates show another great find on Madiun dump: an original DD51 2–8–8–0 Alco Mallet – a scaled down replica of a type that worked over the North American prairies earlier this century. One is depicted protruding out of the undergrowth with an equally moribund DD52 – its European-built relation. The American engine is DD5106 – Alco Works No.58728 of 1919; her relation, DD5205 – Hartmann of Germany Works No.4587 of 1924: see sketch on previous page. Although very similar, these four-cylinder Compound Mallets do have detail differences, particularly the provision of piston valves on all cylinders in the DD52s as against the slide valve operated low-pressure cylinders of the DD51. Though heart-rending to see such magnificent beasts in this condition, their majesty remained apparent, as the pictures clearly depict. I had been told that it was possible to find the last remains of the DD50 Mallets–Alco 1916, but after looking carefully around, including a detailed examination of some huge scrap piles, no evidence was discovered. However the mind boggles as to what might have lain in the centre of such scrap heaps – especially since the works were quite happily overhauling engines nearly 100 years old!

In all, Madiun Works contained ninety locomotives representing no less than thirty-two different classes. I doubt that few, if any, locomotive works in the world today could offer such variety – not to mention contrast.

8. The Last of the 2-4-0s

Plates 1/13/40/41

The 2–4–0 emerged in the 1830's as one of the very early forms of passenger engine. Conceived in Britain, the type was prevalent throughout much of the nineteenth century, both in the home country and abroad. It was one of the earlier loco-motive types used in America where it was quickly superseded by the 4–4–0 but in many other countries the 2–4–0 had, by the mid-nineteenth century, become an important type, especially in Britain, Europe, India and Australia. Undoubtedly the 'pièce de résistance' of all 2–4–0s was 'Hardwicke', a member of Webb's 'Precedent Class' for the London and North Western Railway, which distinguished itself by running the 141 miles from Crewe–Carlisle in 126 minutes – an average speed of 67.2 m.p.h. – as part of the great railway races between the east and west coast routes in 1895. It was inevitable that traffic requirements would, dictate a graduation to the 4–4–0 and, well before the turn of the century this development was almost complete. Of course, many 2–4–0s continued in demoted form well into the twentieth century but for many years now they have been regarded as both obsolete and extinct. However, one notable exception exists with the 1880 built Sharp Stewart 2–4–0s which still operate a small branch line in Central Java. Fourteen were shipped out from Sharp Stewarts' Manchester works between 1880/85; at exactly the same time, the adjacent works of Beyer Peacock were exporting a class of 176 attractive 2–4–0s to the Netherlands Railway.

Classified B50 by the PJKA, only three survived active in 1975 – though several were awaiting shops. Their sole responsibility is the operation of mixed-trains along the branch from Madiun to Ponorogo and onwards to Slahung. Up to Ponorogo they work turn about with the 1912/14 built B53 4–4–0s but only B50s are allowed onwards to Slahung. Although now confined to branch work, the B50s were main line express engines of earlier days and one can imagine them handing over the SS's Jakarta-bound trains at Surakarta to the NIS 4 ft 8½ in. gauge network with its Beyer Peacock 0–4–2s (Plates 10/30). The railway heralded a new age in colonial Java and was a great stimulus to Dutch commerce but few would have believed, that over 90 years later the B50s would still be active – albeit in ailing condition trundling down a partially overgrown branch line.

During part of 1975, the Ponorogo – Slahung section was temporarily closed owing to a lack of operable B50s, but the northern section kept going with one engine hauling three four-wheeled coaches lacking doors, lights, luggage racks, windows and seats – improvised wooden benches being provided as an alternative. In addition one coach in the set, possessed several large holes in its floor through which the weed choked ballast could be seen. Although the authorities at Madiun were able to coerce one of their three steamable B50s into action each day, they had both the wisdom and temerity not to issue any kind of time-table: indeed over a three-day period the train left Madiun prior to dawn on the first day; mid-morning on the second; and early afternoon on the third! Nevertheless to everyone's delight, the train was running.

My footplate journey back into locomotive history was eagerly awaited until shortly before 4.00 one morning, I joined B5014 in Madiun Station. She was piled high with logs and a wall of them stretched from the tender almost to the fire-hole door, virtually separating the driver and fireman; though inconvenient, this arrangement was necessary as the four-wheeled tender had inadequate storage. Standing there in Madiun station, our B50 might have been the subject of a low-key Victorian print; the sombre station awning and first flush of dawn forming a backdrop with the engine sensuously set in the foreground with a full head of steam and rolls of light brown smoke swirling from her long chimney. Steam, leaking badly from her dome, shot out at right-angles with tremendous vitality for a distance of at least thirty feet. Other leaks protruded from both her cylinders and as we started off the engine's front was shrouded in steam; this in turn, poured into the cab through the missing spectacle glasses making driving extremely difficult. The wheezing which set up in her valves was nothing short of dramatic – she sounded like an old London and North Western 'Super D' at its most eloquent. The rear splashers had rusted away on both sides and it was possible to see the wheels going round; this, apart from making conditions dangerous in a small cab, was yet another source by which leaking steam could enter. These leaks soon took their toll on the steam pressure, for although we had started off with a full 9 kg cm^2, this had dropped to 7 kg cm^2 within a mile. The usual fear of steam pressure falling too low for the brake-vacuum did not apply on this journey, since our only method of stopping was the hand-brake of the tender. Disquieting though this thought was, the engine's condition and state of the track positively forbade anything better than a crawl.

Soon after leaving the station, B5014 rumbled her coaches down Madiun's main street; it was just as if someone had opened the doors of the local museum and let the old engine out to run amok in a modern setting. As we passed the market place B5014's whistle echoed and resounded in long shrill shrieks and recumbent figures sleeping on pavements and under stalls were seen to stir. Possibly the number of people sleeping rough did add some credence to the scene – whole families were huddled together, and many betjak boys slept under their conveyances. In a flourish of crimson sparks the iron-clad intruder, having gingerly negotiated the labyrinth of streets, crossed the main Ponorogo road and headed away southwards; miraculously missing two ox-carts – one of which seemed determined to battle over the right of way.

Even a jog of 10 m.p.h. threatened to wind the veteran; every wrench of uneven track seeming to slow her down even more. The rising temperature of morning did nothing to evaporate the steam since the leaks became worse under heavy steaming. In an effort to reconstitute the pressure loss we shut off steam periodically and this caused rich palls of woodsmoke to puther up from the ill-fitting fire-hole doors and crimson tongues of flame licked their way up the backplate with the rapidity of a serpent's fang. Here, with a dome cover ready to rattle its way to the ground, side rods plonking, axle boxes knocking and a jet of steam shooting off at right-angles from the dome, was the last of the 2–4–0s – memories of 'Hardwicke' indeed!

The area around Madiun is noted for sugar plantations and some miles out of town our line met the metals of PG Pagottan – only a main road separating the two. Eventually we caught up a southbound sugar train taking empties back to the plantation. One by one, with an agonising slowness, we overhauled the waggons until we were running alongside the engine whereupon the 2–4–0's lanky curvature contrasted with the fussy green/red Orenstein and Koppel 0–10–0 tender-tank. The combined exhausts of the two engines running side by side were interpolated by exchanged whistle blasts, a strong chime call from the 0–10–1 and a thin piping wail with excellent penetrative qualities from our engine. Low steam pressure caused the B50's whistle to sound like the trilling call of a sandpiper heard across a lonely beach. But despite her superior condition, the 0–10–0TT's tiny wheels were no match for the spinning elegance of the 2–4–0 and soon we drew past only to catch up with another sugar train two miles further on. This was headed by a Borsig built 0–8–0TT in an even smarter green/red livery which greatly discredited the 2–4–0's grimy unlined black. In between the two trains bullet-nosed cars arrogantly snarled past – the strong sunlight glinting off their chromium plated fronts.

Our engine's languid behaviour was typical of PJKA steam, since a rousing whistle is often as much as many can muster. Most are wood burners and they smoke but little, whilst the high temperature usually evaporates any hint of steam they may proffer. Apart from the D52s, few will ever be seen to exert themselves, especially since most heavier duties are diesel-operated. However in B5014's case, almost any deficiency can be forgiven in an engine, which from some angles, looked like a London and North Western Railway Ramsbottom 2–4–0 – low-slung, high-chimneyed and lolloping! On other occasions she resembled a Great North of

Scotland D40 4–4–0, albeit that the B50s are of superior vintage.

Approaching Ponorogo the industrious activities of a track weeding team caught my attention – two men with forks endeavouring to make some impression on the dense green carpet which had lain beneath us all the way from Madiun! As the 2–4–0 swept into the station at Ponorogo it was as if she were heading an important overnight express; with a brief whistle call she rolled over the crossovers and drew to a sedate halt in the platform. She had covered 20 miles in 3 hours – an average speed of 6.66 m.p.h.; 'Hardwicke' during the same month exactly 80 years earlier had covered 141 miles in just over 2 hours – an average speed of 67.2 m.p.h.! But to be fair, B5014 was running when 'Hardwicke' was but a glint in F. W. Webb's eye, and after all, she was the last of the breed.

BRITISH EXPRESS PASSENGER LOCOMOTIVE DEVELOPMENT

– APPROXIMATE EVOLUTIONARY PERIODS

o O o	2–2–2	(Single-wheelers)	1830–1885
oo O o	4–2–2	(Single-wheelers)	1830–1900
oOO	2–4–0		1840–1890
OO o	0–4–2		1840–1890
ooOO	4–4–0		1870–1930
ooOO o	4–4–2	(Atlantic)	1890–1920
ooOOO	4–6–0		1900–1950
ooOOO o	4–6–2	(Pacific)	1920–1955

The above indicates the principal years of building and operating in Britain but may, in general, be applied to many other parts of the world.

9. Cane and Volcanoes

Plates 11/16/29/32/36/39/49

Just outside Madiun on the Ponorogo line is Kanigoro – an
exchange siding from which raw sugar is carried away by the
PJKA. Each evening after sunset either a B50 or B53, runs
down to collect the sugar and bring it into Madiun sidings;
the Ponorogo branch engine is usually assigned for this duty
after it has returned with the daily branch train. One evening,
news came through that the B50 had 'fallen down' – an
Indonesian term for derailment – on its way up from Ponorogo
and so as B5310, a Werkspoor 4–4–0 of 1914, was finding little
to do on the station shunt, it was decided to send her instead.
Running light-engine, we clanked our way noisily through the
town. A sugar train was in the exchange siding and as we
approached a marvellous looking blue tender-tank engine
could be discerned vigorously blowing off. Shown on Plate 32,
she was 'Striklandi' a 1921-built, 700 mm gauge 0–8–0TT
from Orenstein and Koppel. Though belonging to PG
Kanigoro, 'Striklandi' was working for PG Redjo Sari situated
some 15 kilometres southwest of town.

The sight of a main-line 4–4–0 and a 700 mm gauge
0–8–0TT standing side by side brewing up in the moonlight
was enthralling, though within minutes of our arrival 'Striklandi', having completed her shunting, whistled up and set off
on the cross-country journey back to Redjo Sari. We shunted
for a while and had soon assembled a long rake of vans.
Shortly after midnight we were ready to return to Madiun but
the road was not clear. The reason became soon evident as
across the still landscape came the B50's trilling call. A gentle
pounding of cylinders could be heard and a ball of fire became
visible curving its way through darkened palm groves starkly
silhouetted against a moon-lit sky. Sending up a spray of wood
sparks, the 2–4–0 swept past with a nostalgic roll of coupling
rods and a swish of steam. Minutes later we gained the road

and followed on into Madiun.

There are over fifty sugar factories in Java the majority belonging to the State-controlled PNP though just a few remain in private hands; nearly all operate steam locomotives. Over thirty factories are situated in East Java alone; most others being in the central region. Occasionally interconnected, the factories of these two regions provide one of the most fascinating steam networks left in the world today. A splendid range of motive power exists – principally tender-tank engines comprising 0–4–0, 0–4–2, 0–6–0, 0–8–0, 0–10–0 and 0–4–4–0 Mallets. Innumerable different designs and liveries occur, but most engines are of German manufacture between 1900/30 – the years when this industry was being developed under Dutch rule. A 700 mm gauge predominates, though some factories are laid to 600 mm.

Each system usually comprises several lines fanning outwards in different directions from the factory with an average total of around 50 miles of track; frequently engines go 10 miles or more out into the plantation; an estimate of the total sugar-mileage for Java incidentally might be placed at almost 3,000 miles. The average roster of locomotives per factory is eight and it is now known that over 500 PNP steam engines exist; during the milling season virtually all of these were working, this constituting a fundamental difference between the PNP and PJKA, the former being rather better equipped and more efficiently run! An interesting comparison can be made in this respect in that after an extensive survey of the PNP during the 1975 season, covering virtually all factories, of 389 steam engines recorded, no less than 334 were actually in steam. A large percentage, but the actual figure would have been even higher as some engines were far out in the plantations and thus not recorded. Concurrently with this, an extensive, though slightly less comprehensive, survey of the PJKA was conducted which revealed 640 steam engines, but in this instance only 168 were in steam, many of the balance being quite unusuable. However, an amazing total of well over 1,000 engines was recorded for Java which, at a fair guess, would embrace at least 150 different types. Of course, as the PNP sugar-engines are not working all the year round the overhauls and repairs can be sedately undertaken during the off-season, whereas the PJKA attempts to perform a continuous service.

The milling season begins in May and finishes around August–September though in the island's far eastern region it can go on until November. Operations within a system are seldom dull and apart from continuous main line hauls from the plantation, there is a good deal of factory shunting and tripping. Engines leave the shed at dawn bound for the cane fields and return around mid-day; after servicing, the second shift begins and engines leave again, not returning until evening – sometimes after dark. Apart from activities around the factory, there are many plantation junctions from which lines span the fields and the observer, if strategically placed, can see most trains as they converge on to common routes; though sometimes of course, lines radiate away in different directions from the factory itself. Some lines vary from season to season, being slewed in accordance with a cycle of crop plantation and fallow land. Each year Java determines to export sugar, but her vast population consumes all the produce leaving only molasses for selling abroad.

Almost all engines burn bagasse – the natural waste product from cane processing, and though its calorific value is abysmally low, it does provide fuel free of cost. An awful lot is needed to go a short distance and this is why the tender-tank predominates throughout the plantations. Upon reaching the factory, the freshly cut sugar cane is crushed and bagasse is made from the fibres; these are dried out, baled into large cubes and taken to dumps for the locomotives to collect. The construction of tender-tank engines and application of bagasse is well illustrated by Plate 16.

A typical locomotive roster might be seen in the following table on PG Meritjan Nr. Kediri, East Java. (See Plate 49).

RUNNING No.	GAUGE	WHEEL ARRANGEMENT	BUILDER	WORKS No.	DATE
1	700 mm	0–8–0TT	Orenstein Koppel	3349	1909
2	„	„	Borsig	8272	1912
3	„	0 4 2T	Orenstein Koppel	887	1901
4	„	0–4–2TT	„	893	1901
5	„	„	„	10740	1923
6	„	„	„	894	1901
7	„	0–8–0TT	„	1286	1926
9	„	„	„	10433	1923
10	„	0–4–4–0TT MALLET	„	11274	1927

One private concern, the Rejo Agung at Madiun, is represented by Plate 11. This company has a well kept stud of locomotives operating from a roundhouse within the factory confines. However, the 0–4–2T depicted had been derelict for many years and was in such an advanced state of decay that assessment of her origin proved difficult, but she is believed to be American. In absolute contrast comes 'Bromo', a magnificent 0–8–0TT named after a volcano. This engine works for PG Purwodadi and is shown on Plates 16/36, metaphorically living up to her name by erupting fire; she is seen against one of South East Asia's yellow flowering trees. Mount Bromo is a 2,292-metre volcano in East Java famous for its moonlike sand plains dramatically set against its smoking background. Java is world famous for volcanoes and it is the delightful practice of many sugar factories to name their engines after the volcanoes using attractive rectangular nameplates in brass with raised lettering over a red background.

Potent though the plantation engines are when tackling heavy sugar trains, their dimensions are relatively modest and since 'Bromo' is of typical proportions I include the following table of vital statistics:

PG PURWODADI EAST JAVA		LOCOMOTIVE No. 18 'BROMO'	
Builder:	Orenstein & Koppel	Boiler pressure:	12 kg cm^2
Works number:	7379	Horse power:	60
Date:	1914	Tubes:	76
Gauge:	700 mm	Total weight full	
Valve gear:	Stephensons	working order:	20 tons
Cylinders:	200 mm × 340 mm	Fuel:	bagasse
	diameter stroke		

An important sugar town in East Java is Kediri, home of PG Pesantren and PG Meritjan – two large systems operating immaculate yellow liveried steam engines. The time of my visit there coincided with heavy rains; the cane cutters having been forced to abandon their work causing the factories to fall behind in production. Since sugar-milling is controlled with an uncompromising efficiency, an all-out effort was undertaken once the rains stopped and the water level had subsided enough to allow the cutters to resume. Not only were the trains coming in all through the night, but many were overloaded and, struggling every inch of the way. The engines turned the dark skies to crimson with palls of flaming and half consumed bagasse. 'Bringing in the cane by night', is the subject of Plates 29, 49 and I have tried to communicate something of the vital atmosphere which so characterises the milling season.

The Pesantren engines are also named after volcanoes and between the hours of 10.00 p.m. and midnight I went to the yards hoping to see some action. No trains were in when I arrived, the only engine being 'Wilis' – a 1901-built 0–4–2T from Arnold Yung. She was on yard duty pushing the rakes of cane up to the factory crushers. Soon a heavy mainliner

150

arrived behind 'Semeru' – an 0–6–0TT by Orenstein &
Koppel in 1920 – named after Java's highest volcano. She
got a clear road into the sidings and her heavy waggons
rumbled past piled precariously high with cane. Within
minutes the operator's cabin was offered another train from a
different line and so arrived an Orenstein & Koppel, 1925-
built 0–8–0TT delightfully named 'Penanggungan' after a
large mountain. She followed 'Semeru' into the yards and
with two full trains in; 'Wilis' was busy assembling the rakes
as the tender-engines having gone on shed took water and
bagasse before returning to the plantation.

By 11.15 a third freight was offered but this was held outside the factory to allow 'Semeru's' departure with empties
and, with an enormous rake chattering and bowling along
behind her she raised the echoes and thundered away into the
night. Afterwards a heavy coughing exhaust became audible
interspersed by some vigorous slipping; with steam hissing
from her cylinder cocks the labouring engine crawled forwards. It was 'Dieng', an Orenstein & Koppel 0–8–0TT of
1922 – her name commemorating the famous plateau in
Central Java. 'Dieng' was checked again at the factory entrance and stood hissing impatiently until a road was prepared
amid the general yard activity; a busy night indeed!

During the season, PG Pesantren mills 28,000 tons of cane,
an average of around 1,500 tons daily, which, under normal
conditions, means about ten trains per day each hauling
thirty lorries – as the waggons are called – weighing 5 tons
each; a total train weight of around 150 tons. In this part of
Java the campaign lasts from May until November.

Java's dramatic landscape is of obvious interest to the
photographer and next morning I hired a taxi out into the
plantation to meet 'Dieng' which was on its way back with
loads from a line passing near several extinct volcanoes. It was
a race against time as the train was already on its way back
before information had reached the yard. After some ambitious

gesticulations on my part the taxi shot away from Kediri in fine style but before we turned into the plantation an agonising delay for petrol was deemed necessary. Stopping at all was bad enough as the morning sun, though perfect for photography, was being threatened by a steady cloud build-up. But when I saw the method of filling our petrol tank I could have wept, since the garage proprietor, having dutifully assembled his family in a human chain – stretching from inside the garage to our taxi – proceeded to fill a variety of containers with petrol and pass them along the line. Biscuit cans, bottles, jam jars and old oil cans followed one another in grand ceremony. It appeared that the capacity of each container had been recorded on a well-thumbed master card from which the proprietor's wife supervising from an off-side position calculated the total amount of petrol supplied. Any hint of irritation I might have shown was banished instantaneously by an array of beaming faces pointing in my direction. Fascinating as this performance was, I feared that it had cost me the picture but after a hair-raising journey along dusty planatation roads we reached the line and, to my great relief, a planter announced that the train was still on its way. Plate 39, was the result of that morning escapade and it sets the Javan sugar fields into realistic perspective.

Whatever happens on the PJKA, Java will retain its sugar engines for years to come – minimal cost fuel being an important factor. The remarkable combination of industrial and main line steam engines on so small an island as Java constitutes, in my opinion, a steam paradise.

The most modern steam engine in Java is the Leeds-built Hunslet 0–4–2ST of 1971. This interesting engine works for PG Trankil and was the last steam locomotive ever built in Britain. In 1974 a sugar factory on neighbouring Sumatra was desperately scanning the world for three new 150-h.p. steam engines; after some difficulty the order was accepted by a West German firm. Apart from bagasse, this factory had a plenitude of wood in the vicinity and was determined to buy steam locomotives; the company remaining adamant in their refusal of diesels – an honourable precedent for others to follow!

10. The Relics of Cepu

Plates 18/23/31/38/44/54

The sugar systems are highly individualistic and one gets lost in the totality of them so when, with great anticipation, I arrived at Modjokerto I found it a great change to be back amongst mainline engines again. Modjokerto – a junction situated on the southern main line – was said to be operating an old B13 2–4–0T on branch passenger. Not only was I going to be disappointed over seeing it in action, but was about to encounter another series of frustrations over the next few days. Modjokerto depot only contained eleven engines, though seven classes were represented including three B13s and the sole surviving C22 – a gorgeous copper-capped 0–6–0T with a combination of inside/outside frames. This engine, of nineteenth century design, was built for the PSSM (Pasoeroean Stoomtram Mij).

Nothing stirred within the depot, all engines being dead, but as it was a Sunday I remained unsuspecting of the truth. Finding the shedmaster I endeavoured to ascertain from him when a B13 would be running. Communications were inevitably difficult but the chief knew one relevant English word – 'cannot', and pointing to a B13 made up the quaint though highly eloquent phrase, 'cannot stoom' – stoom, of course, being the Dutch word for steam! My closer examination of the B13s revealed their tyres to be badly rusted; the engines were not operable. But, hope springs eternal and I suddenly noticed one B13 was missing – three were on shed

153

and the roster, which the shedmaster produced gave four allocated. Ah, I thought, one must be out on the branch that very day. Indicating the missing engine on his sheet, I pointed to the main line and posed the hopeful question 'has stoom?' Sadly the shedmaster shook his head and uttered one word – 'Madiun'. Immediately I remembered the B13 awaiting shops and, checking back on my number list revealed this to be the engine; doubtless it had gone there months ago and the shedmaster was glumly awaiting its return.

Pointing to the C22 I looked hopefully at my informant. 'Cannot', he uttered and having gone down the complete roster, engine by engine, and elucidated from the shedmaster a succession of 'cannot stoom', 'has nots' and 'no stoom' it eventually dawned on me that every engine was out of action and the depot temporarily closed to traffic. It was tantalising, to say the least, to be confronted by such a range of wonderful engines, each with a defect prohibiting even the most modest performance; a final touch of irony being an abundance of fuel in evidence.

Little less was my disappointment at Babat, when on a fine sunny evening, I entered the neat wooden longhouse situated alongside the north main line from Jakarta–Surabaja. Here were assembled some gorgeous machines, each spotless but none working. I set out below the list of engines in that depot – the 4–4–0s looked, to all intents and purposes, in the prime of their life.

Forlornly they stood, with copper cap chimneys, golden brass domes and safety valves glistening in the clear evening sunlight.

Despondently leaving Babat, I moved to Bodjonegoro – another noted steam centre further along the north main line. Here shortage of wood had silenced yet another magnificent fleet; a pair of B51s stood alongside one another in the shed neither having turned a wheel in months, yet so immaculately cared for they could have been new engines. Several C54

CLASS/ NUMBER	WHEEL ARRANGEMENT	BUILDER	DATE	STATUS
B5117	4–4–0	Hanomag	1903	Repairs-motion down
B5125	,,	Hartmann	1905	Stored
B5302	,,	,,	1912	,,
B5303	,,	,,	1912	,,
C1126	2–6–0T	,,	1890	Dead

4–6–0s were present for working along the main line to Cepu. One C54 stood miserably in the shed yard with about 120 lb of steam in its boiler and a scruffy pile of sundry bits of wood in the tender; this was the shunt engine and providing no heavy movements were necessary she could keep the yard in order.

One expects disappointments when searching out rare machines from bygone times, though nothing ever seems to mitigate the sense of loss and frustration at the actual time. After three depots full of inanimate engines and the main lines which saw little other than diesel-hauled expresses I began to despair. Cepu was next on my itinerary but doubtless the same story would apply there also. The thrilling memories of the B50s and sugar-engines now seemed in the distant past; my musings becoming coloured by pessimism; I thought more of the abandoned DD52s. As if to complete the setting, a violent thunderstorm besotted the town and I was to discover that the hotel roof, when under pressure from heavy rain, leaked abundantly over bed and floor alike. A damp night on a hard bed bode little chance of my dreaming about derelict and dead engines, but such sleep as I had was interrupted at first light by Moslem prayers. The sound of these prayers amplified by loudspeakers situated in various parts of the town was to say the least eerie; but combined with the hubbub of awakening cats and dogs, the early morning miscellany of sound that greeted me effectively prevented any further chance of sleep.

On my arrival at Cepu, a gleaming C12 welcomed me to the station, and palls of smoke could be seen rising above the shed. Here at last, was a depot which had managed to keep up on repairs, obtain sufficient fuel and, against all the odds, succeed in maintaining a small fleet of engines in service. No less than five were active and, true to Javan traditions, each was of a different class. The C12 was sharing shunting work with a D15 – both lone examples of their type found active. The D15s are sufficient to inspire anyone's imagination, being long, outside-framed tank-engines with Klein-Linder end axles to make their wheelbase flexible. Most have gorgeous yellow domes and their outside cylinders are topped with voluptuously curved steam pipes which contrast vividly with the harsh rectangular form of their enormous blood-red buffer-beams.

In essence, the D15s reminded me of the Mersey Railway's classic 0–6–4T 'Cecil Raikes' now preserved in Britain and memories flooded back to the time when I visited Heanor Colliery in Derbyshire many years ago when this engine was working there in industrial service. The Klein Linders, as the PJKA engines are known, have the same heavy elongated, almost clumsy, appearance but nevertheless are highly impressive machines as witness Plates 23, 44 and 54. The five D15s all came from Hanomag in 1931 and were built for the Semerang Joana Stoomtram (SJS); their design was almost identical with eleven earlier engines introduced in 1913 and classified D10. The initial six D10s were also destined for the SJS but the other five, delivered from Hartmann in 1914/15, belonged to the Serajoedal Stoomtram (SDS). Many 'Klein Linders' have been altered to 0–6–2Ts by the removal of their rear-connecting rod whilst many, in common with 'Cecil Raikes' have stovepipe chimneys; fortunately the engine illustrated has the more elegant copper-lipped variety.

CLASS/No.	WHEEL ARRANGEMENT	BUILDER	DATE	STATUS
B5110	4–4–0	Hanomag	1902	Derelict
B5111	4–4–0	Hanomag	1902	Derelict
C1206	2–6–0T	Hartmann	1895	Station shunts
C1224	2–6–0T	,,	1896	Repairs
C2830	4–6–4T	Henschel	1921	Dead
C2835	4–6–4	Hartmann	1921	Dead
C2846	4–6–4T	Esslingen	1921	Working main line
C2852	4–6–4T	,,	1921	Dead
C5104	4–6–0	Beyer Peacock	1912	Dead
C5106	4–6–0	,,	1912	Dead
C5108	4–6–0	,,	1912	Working ballast/ P.W. Trains
C5417	4–6–0	,,	1922	Working main line
C5419	4–6–0	,,	1922	Repairs
D1505	0–8–0T	Hanomag	1931	Yard shunts

With a C12/D15 on station shunt, the train workings fell to larger engines, and duties along the main line to the junction further west at Gambringan were undertaken either by a C28 4–6–4T or C54 4–6–0. Special ballast and permanent way trains within the area were being run by a C51, one of ten colonial looking ex NIS 4–6–0s with large windshields. The windshields completely alter the C51s' appearance, though basically they are very similar to classes C52/4. Another particularly interesting engine at Cepu was No.C2835 which had been converted into a highly potent-looking tender engine; this impressive machine, attached to a semi-stream-lined tender, had lost her side-tanks but retained her smoke deflectors. A pair of very derelict B51 4–4–0s stood outside – one of them is illustrated on Plate 18.

A complete list of engines at Cepu is given above.

Although no one individual can hope to really solve the PJKA's operational difficulties, one does gain the impression that activities around Cepu are due in no small part to the shedmaster whose enthusiasm for the engines and his work has somehow kept the trains running; this depot, above all, is a credit to the entire system.

Cepu also boasts a splendid forestry railway laid to 3 ft 6 in. gauge with some 150 miles of track. In addition to 0–10–0T/ 0–6–0WTs of purely industrial design, this system also possesses several ex PJKA classes including an 0–6–0 Tram Engine. The Perusahan Kohutanan, as the forestry concern is known, is exceptional amongst Indonesian industrial establishments in having a gauge identical with the PJKA's; it is unfortunate that Java's plantation lines are incompatible with the PJKA; so forbidding any obsolete or superfluous main-liners from finding a second home.

11. The Jatibarang Pumpers

Plate 7

Jatibarang is rather an insignificant town whose conglomeration of disjointed buildings line narrow streets which, within yards of their prime, peter into obscurity through the surrounding palm-groves. The town's situation on the north main line affords some national status as does the branch line to Indramaju though I was shocked to find the latter overgrown with weeds and temporarily abandoned. Here, at last, I had tracked down the only active B13 2–4–0T. She was B1304 – Hanomag 1885, and was subsheded out from Cirebon for shunting. The only other occupant of Jatibarang's longshed was a B50 2–4–0 from Sharp Stewart in 1881 – the engine formerly used on the branch.

Both locomotives however, spend the majority of their time as stationary pumping engines – one for oil, the other water – serving both railway and communal needs. In fact, on the day of my arrival, the B50 was actively pumping water and although the B13 was idle, the depot chargehand – who knew no English – pointed vigorously in her direction and proclaimed 'pumpa lok'!

The 2–4–0 tank engine is an important form in locomotive history; it was used extensively for branch and suburban trains in many parts of the world from the mid-nineteenth century onwards – nearby Japan's first steam locomotive being a 2–4–0T in 1871. Indonesia's B13s represent the finest of old traditions; one could imagine these period pieces puffing in and out of Broad Street some hundred years ago. All were delivered from Hanomag in 1885 and discovery of an active engine made full recompense for the disappointment at Modjokerto. Thus in Jatibarang were 92-year-old 2–4–0 survivors; one a tender engine; the other a tank. The photograph depicting these rarities is indeed an historical one; the engines, caught either side of semaphore signals, are set against a typical Javan sky and tropical vegetation; the scruffy B13 is greatly relieved by the colourful State flags fluttering on her buffer beam.

The Javan adventure had read like the pages of a history book and photographing that pair of engines made a splendid finale to my visit to Jatibarang. Again, though as a railway historian involved in the everyday world of Indonesia I could scarcely ignore the human element. My last memories of the town are of a D5 2–8–2 running into the station absolutely smothered with people. Several freight trains had passed through with illegal loads of passengers, but now with only an engine available, somewhat unreasonable demands had been made on available space. I had been able to identify the class of the engine only by its wheels; no other part of its anatomy was visible other than the chimney top and sides of the fender. Well over 200 people were clinging to the engine; had the scene been staged for a film, it could hardly have been more hilarious.

Some 300 people had closely watched my activities in Jatibarang. In shed yards they had swarmed over engines chanting 'portret', 'portret', 'portret'; only a peremptory 'minggir' – stand aside – made photography possible. The cameras confronting the 2–4–0s utterly baffled the onlookers; they were unable to equate any form of logic in my actions and proffered nothing but incredulous stares; but when the time came to move on, I had no energy to even try and explain.

12. *The Japanese Engines of Taiwan*

Plates 15/56

One hundred miles off the Chinese mainland lies Taiwan; a luxurious yet rugged island about the size of Holland. In 1895 China's defeat in the Sino–Japanese war led to the island being occupied by the Japanese – a state of affairs which existed until 1945 when reunion with China was made. This reunion was short-lived, since four years later, in 1949, the Communists took over the mainland and the National Government under Chiang Kai Shek was forced to retreat to Taiwan. It remains today as a refuge for the free Chinese – the country regarding itself as being in a permanent state of war with mainland China.

One might expect Taiwan to reflect a very cosmopolitan locomotive stock, such as existed on the mainland. However, under the occupation, Japanese ideas were supplanted and the main line engines became virtually identical with Japanese stock. Taiwan's 3 ft 6 in. gauge, though compatible with Japan's, was actually begun prior to the occupation; the first section being opened in 1891: this was in marked contrast with the standard 4 ft 8½ in. gauge on the Chinese mainland. But almost the entire network was laid under Japanese rule and today the Taiwan Government Railway (TGR) consists of a west coast main line running the island's length and a much shorter east coast section laid to 2 ft 6 in. gauge. The first important class of engine delivered for the west coast line was ten Avonside 2–4–0Ts in 1895; one is preserved in the capital – Taipei.

The TGR now have an excellent and densely used railway system with regular diesel-hauled expresses running up to and over 60 m.p.h. Such steam as remains is all on the west coast route; the east line being entirely diesel. Fascinating as the TGR steam engines are, the island can muster other delights, particularly the world famous Ali Shan logging railway with its Shay locomotives. Lesser known are the many sugar lines situated especially in the south western area. Here, many steamers survive on a dense network of interconnected plantation systems which lie between the west coast line and the sea. Over 1,000 miles of track is in operation, connecting at intermittent points, with the TGR. Now under the auspices of the Taiwan Sugar Corporation, these industrials are of either German or Japanese origin – although the Japanese began developing the sugar industry early this century, many engines were obtained from Germany, but in more recent times Japanese engines have begun to infiltrate. The 2 ft 6 in. gauge – common to both the Ali Shan and sugar networks – is in unison with Japan's narrow gauge railways.

Over recent years Japan's steam locomotives have come to be regarded as a highly pleasing school of engines – moderately proportioned, conventional, yet varied in design and distinctive in appearance. Two separate phases can be seen; the European period dating up to 1919 and the period from then on. Plate 15 gives some indication of this by showing a 2–8–0/2–6–0 of European – even British appearance – against an all purpose 2–8–2 of typical latter-day Japanese styling. Over the last 60 years the 2–6–0, 2–8–0, 4–6–2 and 2–8–2 have predominated – the types now bringing steam operations in Japan to a close. The truly native designs of 4–6–2, 2–8–2 and various tank classes are of imposing appearance and quite different from anything else in the world; in visual terms they are as individualistic as the German Reichsbahn standards.

Taiwan received many important Japanese designs: six predominantly working there today; three of them being shown in Plate 15. On the left is a heavy, beefy-looking consolidation of the European phase, the TGR Class DT 850 (Japanese National Railways – JNR, Class 9600). These are nicknamed 'Old Oxen' on account of their heavy plodding manner and appearance. Of British styling, they were first introduced in 1913 and have served as important freight and shunting engines ever since; very large numbers being built. Apart from working some main line freights, the 'Old Oxen' can be found on shunting work at several centres along the west coast line; they also remain hard at work in Japan. In the centre is a Mogul – TGR Class CT 150 (JNR Class 8620) – a nicely-styled period piece. These were the first of three important Mogul classes built for Japan and are ubiquitous on light mixed duties – though during World War I they were the standard express passenger locomotives until being super-seded by the C51 Pacific in 1919. First built in 1914, the CT150s look rather like the Southern Railway's 'N' class Moguls of exactly the same period; the dimensions of the two types would, I imagine, be very similar. On the right is a TGR Class DT650 (JNR Class D51) Mikado – an important class of 1,100 mixed-traffic 2–8–2s built between 1936–1945 which epitomise the Japanese style. The D51s are a modern version of the 380 D50 2–8–2s built over the years 1923/31. Now the most numerous steam class in Taiwan and Japan, the D51s, along with the Pacifics, have boxpok cast, steel-coupled wheels and enormous windshields.

This impressive line-up was made at Hsinchu, an important depot which provided me with my first real sighting of Japanese engines – five different classes were present. After seeing a predomination of diesels on the run down from Taipei, it was refreshing to discover an active stud of steam engines smoking and hissing in the half-round house. The 'Old Oxen' stood protruding from the depot when, on the next road but one came a D51 2-8-2 – the pair made a fine comparison – but when the 8620 Mogul slipped into place between them – having been temporarily taken off station shunt for attention to a broken tender spring – a fine trio was achieved.

Amid the excitement of seeing the three engines boiling up side by side, my attention turned casually to an incoming train from the south; this, to my delight was headed by a TGR Class CT270 (JNR Class C57) Pacific. Never will I forget that first sighting of a Japanese Pacific. The Pacific is traditionally an express type, many sleek and racy looking designs having been prepared, yet the C57s seems to be an 'identikit' for the entire breed. Their long, low-slung, rounded boiler with the firebox behind the coupled wheels set against enormous windshields and large spinning boxpok driving wheels 5 ft 9 in. in diameter make them rakish thoroughbreds built for speed in the best of Pacific traditions. The generous loading gauge allows them to have tall stovepipe chimneys and a large housing containing dome and sandbox – elements which accentuate the engines' 'slender-waisted' appearance. I was so thrilled with this engine that I ran up the line to the far end of the station to watch her leave but, to my great joy, she uncoupled and slid silently back through the station bound for the shed.

Japan has become renowned for her Pacifics; the type first being introduced there in 1919 with the now extinct two-cylinder C51. Two classes of three-cylinder Pacifics were built, but in later designs, the C55 (1935) and C57 (1937), a reversion was made to two-cylinders. The C57s are a development of the original C51 and building continued after the war. They are found on passenger and freight workings in both countries, though inevitably they have, of late, been relegated to duties of lesser importance.

Thus with Pacifics on passenger, D51 Mikados on freight, Moguls on station pilot and three dusty looking 'Old Oxen' Consolidations on yard shunt and local goods work, Hsinchu proved an excellent centre – the town being well laced with smoke and chime whistles. But for all this, possibly an even greater attraction lay further south at Chia Yi – a town set deep in sugar plantation country. Here, apart from a magnificent Pacific allocation was the Ali Shan logging railway – a last haunt of the Shay engine and one of the world's most famous steam worked railways.

Very few passenger trains are steam-hauled between Hsinchu and Chia Yi but a little planning enabled me to ride behind a C57 over the 'mountain route' – the west coast main line splits over a short section, one part following the coast, the other running inland; the two sections later rejoin. We had seven coaches and two luggage vans. The van doors were left open to aid ventilation and, by sitting in the entrance, I could see the magnificent terrain and the engine ahead as it forged its way round curves, over viaducts and into tunnels. Some viaducts spanned enormous pebble-strewn river beds containing the merest trickle between small pools of water, but their powerful supports and girders spoke much of the raging torrents encountered in the wet season. Several times during this hot journey green tea was served in the traditional Chinese manner, along with a standard meal of rice, pork, egg and pickles served hot in special aluminium containers – complete with chopsticks!

Early this century, the Japanese decided to exploit the magnificent Cedar Stands which lie in the mountains behind Chia Yi – the Ali Shan railway being constructed for this purpose. The scheme was known to be ambitious, but the hazards encountered once work had begun surprised even the most hardened engineers. The 42-mile line included some unbelievably spectacular works; spirals, switchbacks, awesome viaducts spanning bottomless ravines and tunnels: the climb

DIMENSIONS

	TGR CT 270 Class	TGR DT 650 Class
	(JNR C57 Pacific)	(JNR D51 Mikado)
Cylinders	$19\frac{3}{4} \times 26$	$21\frac{3}{4} \times 26$
Driving Wheel Diameter	5 ft 9 in.	4 ft 7 in.
Boiler Pressure	228 lbs per sq. in.	200 lbs per sq. in.
Tractive Effort	28,000 lbs	37,500 lbs.

to 7,600 ft was achieved by 120 bridges and 50 tunnels! In passing, one might make a comparison with the notable 332 mile-long journey from Mombasa–Nairobi. (*Steam Safari*, Vol. III). This line climbs 5,000 ft, but the Ali Shan achieves a considerably greater altitude in one-eighth of the distance! Two and three truck Shay engines from Lima still perform over the Ali Shan today. It will be seen that Chia Yi is the best steam centre on Taiwan – especially when one considers the sugar lines in the immediate vicinity.

Plate 56 was taken at Chia Yi depot just before CT282 went off shed one Sunday morning to take a southbound passenger. Emitting rich palls of coal smoke, the Pacific backed on to its ten coach train and – standing there surrounded by passengers in a modern station – she vividly evoked the days when steam ruled the main line and the Pacific was the prime power. Easily but gently, the thoroughbred got her train on the move; the packed coaches – with people standing all along corridors – rolled past. Once the inertia was overcome the Pacific 'bit' in a more pronounced way sending grey shrouds of exhaust into the sunny skies as she headed away southwards along a dead straight track stretching for miles. After about half a mile the blazing heat threw a curtain of haze over the express; the glaring light shimmered vibrantly and the train began to melt into abstraction. It was wonderful to stand on the platform and watch the departure: after five minutes the Pacific was still discernible as a misty speck on the steel ribbons stretching to infinity across the flat landscape southwards from Chia Yi.

13. Negros - the enchanted island

It is sad that our thoughts and dreams of romantic islands are invariably confined to a fantasy world. In wistful escapism, many of us foster dreams of remote sunny islands where a mystical harmony can be found; where a magical balm will dissolve stress and care, and where we may enjoy the rest of our days in warm sunshine and contentment. The search for absolute peace involves us all although in real life it inevitably recedes from our grasp.

I would seldom disagree with those who hastily spell out the innate dangers of such day dreams. Thus it came as something of a shock when, almost unwittingly, I found my dream island; a haven of peace which provided me with an almost frightening sense of harmony and fulfilment.

It was as if one night my fairy-godmother had appeared and asked me to describe a perfect existence. I might well have replied, 'give me a beautiful wife and a sunny island with golden beaches and a blue ocean. Fill the island with people, handsome in appearance and temperate in disposition; scatter the landscape with exotic fruits, flowers and birds; allow cascading water to tumble through wooded valleys; and dominate this paradise with an enormous smoking volcano. Then, fill the island with fabulous steam engines – the finest imaginable – and let them puff, moan and cry amid all the beauty you have created. That, fairy-godmother, is my perfect existence!'

One October evening shortly before dusk, a small silver

plane circled over Bacolod Airport on the remote Philippine island of Negros. Glinting in the late sunlight, the plane left the cloud flecked heights, arched round in long sweeping curves, and approached the short runway; down below a loudspeaker was announcing the arrival of the evening flight from Manila. The plane bumped to a halt in front of the small terminal building and I stepped down into a dream – my wish come true. Overpowered by an indescribable feeling of elation, I began the adventure of a lifetime.

Over the remaining pages of this volume I hope to justify such a claim; Negros is one of the most beautiful places on earth and, in my opinion, it holds the most incredible steam locomotives left today. If engines and landscape were the sum total of the island's allure it would be exciting enough, but the population consists of the most warm hearted, generous and hospitable people imaginable; in brief, Negros *is* a veritable paradise.

Sugar is the Philippines' principal dollar earner and many important plantations are situated on Negros. The island, fourth largest in the Philippine Archipelago, is about 100 miles long against 30 miles wide. Discovered by Magellan for the Western world in 1521, the Philippines became a colony of Spain until 1898 when authority over them was transferred to the U.S.A. Over the ensuing years, until independence in 1946, American influence was extensive with tremendous development taking place. A vivid reflection of the Americanisation is found in the locomotives and the vast colony of old Lima, Alco and Baldwin engines working on Negros is noteworthy – such engines having virtually disappeared elsewhere with the possible exception of South America. A Baldwin Mallet, Lima Shays and a host of other exotica – both tank and tender – proliferate, in the widest range of colours, over rail systems ranging from good, bad, to positively lethal! During the 1920's, Henschel of Germany conducted an extensive campaign for their products in the South East Asian market and some European infiltration resulted but the Philippine motive power remains – to the delight of rail connoisseurs the world over – principally American. As the sugar field engines of Indonesia orientate wholly towards Europe, those of the Philippines follow New World practice.

About ten sugar systems operate steam on the island; most are laid to 3 ft 0 in. gauge though one of the systems, the Victorias Milling Co. has a 2 ft 0 in. gauge, whilst another, Lopez Sugar Central – which numbers amongst its roster two Lima Shays – is laid to a 3 ft 6 in. gauge. Apart from the diverse steam workings, horse drawn railtrams known as Wagonetas run in parts of the island. However, the pièce de résistance is undoubtedly The Insular Lumber Co., a classic logging railway in the finest American traditions.

The sugar milling season on Negros lasts from October to April, though Victorias Milling – noted principally for its Henschels – works nearly all the year round as, of course, does Insular Lumber. But let us take a more detailed look at the atmosphere and intrigue of the three most important systems: The Hawaiian–Philippine Co.; Ma-Ao Sugar Central; and The Insular Lumber Co. Collectively, these systems provide a unique and varied group of engines.

14. The Red Dragons

Plates 2/8/24/28/35/43/47/51

After a night in Bacolod, I journeyed a few miles along the coast to the great sugar plantation of the Hawaiian Philippine Co. – one of the island's larger sugar concerns well-known for having some splendid green Baldwins with huge cabbage stack chimneys. The factory, set deep in the plantation, was surrounded by a community known as the company compound; here, houses, shops, a bank, a hospital and other amenities provided self-contained living for the employees. I was made to feel welcome and within minutes of my arrival at the main gates, was being taken to see the company administrator Mrs L. Arceo Samaniego – a personage well endowed with traditional Filipino charm. She told me, 'we in the Philippines are the most hospitable people in the world.' This remark was well borne out over the ensuing weeks.

Anxious to see the engines, I was soon being escorted through the compound to the depot. I had been under the impression that there were no red engines on Negros. I had often thought this a little strange, especially as the plantations are predominantly green and, if only for safety reasons, red engines would have stood out in better relief. Imagine my amazement when upon reaching the yard, an immaculate Baldwin 0–6–0 was seen done out in red with yellow lining; in the background stood another engine in comparable condition. The entire roster had been painted red just two months previously and, as the season was just beginning, the engines were spotless – having laid dormant under repair since April. Previously, all Hawaiian Philippine engines had been green, but on account of their being difficult to see out in the cane fields, the manager had given instructions for them to be painted red – an action which greatly assisted the photographer, too!

The locomotives looked like a collection put together as a tourist attraction; like big painted toys with more than a hint of fairground engines about them. It was hard to believe that they were part of a large company operating stringent production and economic control. Referred to as 'Dragons', all engines were in radio contact with the control office, so enabling their movements throughout the plantation to be properly co-ordinated. Although milling had just begun, the Dragons were hard at work with three shifts daily; out at 8.00 a.m. returning 1 p.m., leaving again at 3.00 p.m. until 7.00

Dragon Number	Wheel Arrangement	Builder	Date
1	0–6–0	Henschel	1923
2	"	Baldwin	1919
3	"	"	1920
4	"	"	"
5	"	"	"
6	"	"	"
7	"	"	1928
8	0–6–2T	"	1924
9	0–6–2T	"	1916

p.m., departing again at 9.00 p.m. and coming back around 3.00 a.m. the following morning: seven different lines being worked, each with a different name. No cane was loaded on Sundays – a day put aside for servicing and cleaning.

The company began in 1920 and in the previous year two 10-in. Baldwin 0–6–0s were delivered numbered 1/2 (Plate 35). Once work was under way, Baldwins supplied some straightforward enlargements with 12-in. cylinders – nos 3–6 (Plate 28). In 1923, an engine was built by Henschel – presumably as a result of their far eastern sales campaign. Ostensibly, she was identical with the Baldwins but had 13-in. cylinders enclosed in rectangular casings in contrast with the characteristically rounded American versions; other minor differences divulge this engine's origin and make her something of a pretender. The German engine is a 20-tonner, as against the respective 10- and 18-ton Baldwins. A further engine, numbered 7 and identical with nos. 3–6 came from Baldwin in 1928 and the total complement was made up 20 years later when the two 15-ton 0–6–2Ts were transferred from Hawaii (Plate 35). The original Baldwin 10-in. 0–6–0 has since disappeared and her number is now carried by the Henschel. All, except No 2, have a driving wheel diameter of

2 ft $10\frac{3}{4}$ in. Dragon 6's roller-bearing tender gives an infinitely superior ride when compared with the brass-bearing tenders of other engines; especially over rough track.

When the Japanese occupied the island during World War II, Dragons 1–7 were hidden to prevent them being destroyed or taken away. When the invasion was imminent, the engines were steamed up and run to the end of a mountain line; a special extension track was then laid to lead the engine into deep undergrowth; this effectively hid them from sight by land or air. After they had literally been steamed into the scrub, the extension track was lifted and all signs covered up. Here the Dragons remained safely for 3 years – no Japanese patrol ever locating them.

It was enthralling to be out with these engines as they tripped around the plantation; the entire system seemed like an enormous adventure railway being run solely for pleasure: a few words on the accompanying pictures might serve to communicate something of the magical atmosphere.

Plate 8. On a morning of diffused sun light, two labourers circled an area of plantation from which cane had been cut a few days previously; all that remained were the dry brown leaves lying several inches thick on the ground. The men dropped lit torches into the field; the leaves instantaneously ignited – an absence of rain having rendered them as dry as timber. Crimson sheets of flame shot upwards in minor explosions. Crackling like distant machine-gun bursts, the fiery tornado swept across the plantation within seconds, producing a liquid heat haze. Small mammals and the occasional bird darted in advance of the encroaching flames; those unable to escape becoming part of the blackened and charred expanse which, like the depredations of a victoriously advancing army, lay behind the front-line. With the blaze at its height, a locomotive whistle rang out and, looking through the flames to the field's edge, I witnessed Dragon 6 rolling by with a trainload of empty waggons. A less careful observer might have assumed that an errant spark from the engine had caused the fire, for despite the Dragon's elaborate spark-arresting chimney such happenings are not infrequent during dry periods.

Plates 24, 28. The morning had dawned clear after a night of rain and although cumulus cloud was beginning to form, the sun was shining brilliantly as we left the yard on Dragon 6 with empties for the Magasa line. Our engine, freshly over-hauled, made good progress and soon we were out in the wilds surrounded by acres of cane on either side. After about 8 miles, a radio message ordered us to sidetrack – a factory-bound train needed to pass. Steaming into a passing loop we reset the points, put a green flag by the trackside and left the main line clear. The crew took this opportunity to have lunch and, sitting alongside our quietly simmering engine, a marvellous meal of fresh shrimps and rice was spread out on the grass; a repast completed with soft fruits and locally grown coffee.

A throaty exhaust, delivered crisp and clear from perfectly set valves, heralded the mainliner's approach. The engine's copper bell clanged with a lovely musical resonance followed by a gloriously undulating wail of chime whistling – a shimmering sound reminiscent of Casey Jones's famous 'Whippoorwill Whistle'. The engine was working hard, yet a gentle sigh of steam could be heard issuing from her safety valves. The rapturous sounds drew closer until Dragon 4 loomed into view; the sounds, combined with the engine's appearance, produced a feeling of ethereality. She swept past oscillating violently over the rough track and, for several minutes afterwards, her bell and chime whistle remained audible, animating the silent plantation with golden tones. We reset the points and continued our journey. Plate 28 was made whilst propelling six empties into a loading bay – the muddy and swollen river bearing testimony to the previous night's rain. Plate 24, made later that day, sees us scuttling homewards with a loaded train against an ominously dusky sky – the tail of a typhoon which

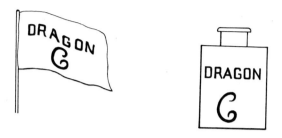

Flag and drinking water can of 'Dragon 6'

was later to cause considerable damage on nearby Luzon Island.

Plate 35. The fairground atmosphere is really brought out by this pair at the factory interchange; the o–6–o having just arrived with a train as the Hawaiian o–6–2T prepares to assemble it. Plate 47. All the company's engines burn bagasse, but at the beginning of a campaign there is not always sufficient to go round thus certain engines temporarily consume oil: the necessary tanks being sunk into their tenders; stovepipe chimneys are also applied. It is difficult to believe that Dragon 7 is identical with her cabbage-stacked sisters, so different does she appear on account of her stovepipe chimney; Dragon 7's fluted stovepipe contrasting sharply with the slim one on Dragon 5.

Plate 51. 9 p.m. on weekday evenings finds all the engines within the factory confines. The shed is a hive of activity; watering, oiling up, minor repairs, bagassing and other sundry duties needing to be completed before the fleet can leave for the plantation. In the transport manager's office, a trip/collection schedule is being finalised after a detailed collation of information from all parts of the system upon the whereabouts of waggons, both loaded and empty. Friendly exchanges between crews, the odd driver or brakeman on the carpet over a derailment, frenzied phone calls from planters demanding urgent delivery of empties and countless other routine incidents, all culminate into an exciting flux characteristic of the five-month campaign.

By 10 p.m. all is quiet and the Dragons assemble at the head of their trains; one by one they disappear into the far corners of the 100-mile railroad network; another night-shift is under way.

15. *Adventures at Ma Ao*

Plates 3/14/20/42/50

The motley array of dead engines which greeted me at Ma Ao Sugar Central's ramshackle depot, looked like the contents of a scrap yard; it seemed hardly credible that in a few days time, when milling began, they would all be hard at work. None had seen paint in years and those parts of their anatomy not rusted over were covered by a multitude of faded, cracked and peeling hues: it was blissful decrepitude. Their balloon-stacked chimneys were echoed by battered oil barrels; these contained sand and were placed on the boiler top – each barrel having a corrugated iron roof to keep out water. To ensure the bagasse remained dry during heavy rains, the tender sides were also sheeted up with corrugated iron, held in place with bits of string and wire. The active fleet was four Alco 2–6–0s; two of them in blue livery with yellow tenders taken from withdrawn Baldwin 0–6–2s.

Pride of the line was No.5, an engine in a truly chaotic state, her chimney, smokebox, sand barrels and warning bell were all a blaze of rust contrasted against a silver boiler, black wheels, green cab and yellow tender; and, if this was not enough, lettering on the cabside was white and red on the tender: with the exception of blue, all major facets of the

174

spectrum were in evidence (Plate 42). The condition of these machines makes an amazing comparison with those of the Hawaiian Philippine Co. some miles further north.

My first trip was with No. 1 – a blue Alco 2–6–0 shown in Plate 50. We had to take five 30-ton vans containing raw sugar from the factory up to the coastal wharf on the Pulupandan Line. The sugar was for export to China and America. Under easy steam, we ran the downhill journey of some 10 miles and, upon reaching the wharf ran round our train and propelled the vans above disposal ducts set between the track. Once in position, the waggon bottoms were capsized and the sugar dropped through on to a wide conveyor belt taking it to an immense warehouse.

The raw sugar – looking like Demerara, was good to eat, especially when meals were missed on account of long rail trips and whilst the Alco was assembling empties, I took an opportunity to see inside the warehouse. It was a vast structure like an aircraft hanger and inside were 50,000 tons of sugar – mountains, upon mountains of it – glowing a dull brown under the soft warehouse lights; it was an unforgettable spectacle. From this warehouse the sugar continues on its journey by conveyor into overhead hoppers at the quayside and here the produce is dropped into the ships' holds; some boats being capable of taking cargoes of 10,000 tons.

After No. 1 had assembled nine 10-ton empties, we received instructions to tow back a 40-ton diesel locomotive which had failed earlier that afternoon, and before collecting the diesel, I was amazed to see our driver putting off three of the empty vans. He explained that owing to No. 1's poor steaming capacity, the inefficiency of bagasse as fuel, and the adverse grades on the return journey, he felt a train weighing 100 tons would be the limit. Although I never seriously doubted his judgement I was amazed that we could not take the full 130 tons; I suggested that we tried to take the complete train – we would get through somehow. He was tempted, we might

175

indeed he admitted, but she was steaming so badly he feared we would stall. How right he was, for having dropped the three empties and settled for the 100-ton train, it soon became evident that we were in difficulty. Our two firemen, one breaking up the bagasse cubes, the other avidly firing, worked at a tremendous pace. The fuel exploded and ignited like straw the second it reached the firebed and before the engine could glean any appreciable calorific value, half of the wretched stuff was flung partially consumed from the chimney. The pressure gauge flickered precariously low despite a level track.

A long and arduous climb lay ahead preceded by a short downhill stretch; the best we could do was to make a run at the bank and hope for the best. I began to help the two firemen as, soaked in sweat from effort and the fire's blinding heat, we worked frenziedly; little improvement appearing on the pressure-gauge but at least we prevented it from dropping any lower. Our driver eased the regulator to the fully open position, jerkily No.1 responded; the charge was on. A tremendous amount of bagasse is needed even for a short, easy journey and although it is inefficient as well as a possible cause of igniting fires in the surrounding countryside – hence the enormous spark-arresting chimneys – it is preferred to imported coal from Japan or Australia; the locally-mined coal from neighbouring Cebu Island being of such poor quality that it has to be mixed with copra and firewood.

No.1's frenzied exhaust beats grew slower as the grade took its toll; she sounded as if she were being wound backwards into slow motion. Each agonising gasp, produced by a weakened piston thrust, demanded our constant attention; the pressure gauge sagged and the driver stood ready to apply the tender handbrake lest we stopped. With an agonising roar No.1 topped the grade and the factory lights became visible far across the landscape. Now, with the grade in our favour, we merrily bowled along and the boiler pressure surged towards its zenith; the driver giving a smile of relief over those empty cars left at Pulupandan wharf.

Part of the machinery at Ma Ao factory is steam-powered and enormous cylinders drive a giant fly wheel; the poignant blatancy of this apparatus conjuring up childhood memories of seeing large spinning steam locomotive wheels for the first time. Leaving the factory buildings shortly after 1.00 a.m., I joined the illustrious No.5 preparing to take the 2.00 a.m. departure along the Cutcut Line. I found the engine being loaded with bagasse from the yard dump. Our journey was to take us many miles away to the base of an active volcano; steam engines being preferred on the mountain lines as they have a better braking capacity than diesels.

At 2.15 a.m. all was ready, and running tender first propelling thirty empties, we passed from the dimly lit factory yard into the remoteness of the plantation. I climbed up on to No.5's tender; it was a crystal clear night and a myriad stars gazed down benignly from a dark sky washed with cobalt blue. Far ahead, in stark silhouette, lay the volcano – its base merging into obscurity. With such an inspiring vista I felt the world to be at peace. We stopped unexpectedly at a loading siding and I was called down from the tender; coffee was being served nearby. The brakemen, who ride on the waggons, appeared and together we followed No.5's crew through a darkened grove of trees to a clearing where, from a long wooden hut a woman and girl were dispensing glasses of thick black locally grown coffee. We all sat together on crude benches beneath the trees and cigars were passed round. Peace reigned supreme.

Half an hour later we set off again and soon our climb towards the volcano began, No.5's exhaust sharpening as shrouds of flaming bagasse puthered skywards. Miles ahead a headlamp was discernible curving round the hillside; it was No.3 which had left the factory an hour before us and was sharing the same line for some distance.

Resuming my position on the tender I was just in time to see our brakeman frantically waving a red lamp from the leading waggon; the lamp wobbled precariously for a few seconds and then suddenly darted off at an angle and disappeared – the brakeman had obviously thrown himself clear! There was a rending crash of metal ahead: a full brake application caused me to lose balance and the train shuddered to a halt. Eight waggons were off the road, some veering away at right-angles deep into the sugar cane. I wrongly concluded that this set-back would take hours to correct, so chaotic did the derailment appear, yet in 30 minutes we were rerailed by a combination of ingenuity and rerailing clamps specially carried on all engines. Often several derailments will occur on one journey and the alacrity of their correction is amazing (Plate 14).

The volcano loomed ever closer and as we pounded our way towards it the first flush of dawn appeared; the sun was to rise immediately above the mound. The ginger sunlight, ever increasing in brilliance, caused our side of the volcano to change into a successive progression of purples until, finally bursting over from behind the volcano, the sun lit the grey lava ridden wastes revealing their true perspective (Plate 20). This volcano, which dominates the island, erupts flame and smoke each April.

We had several loading sidings to service and there were many full waggons, from various growers, awaiting our collection. The type of cane and its juice content varies from grower to grower, each waggon load having to be weighed separately and the juice independently accounted at the factory. Needless to say, the company's analysts are not allowed to know which particular grower's cane they are assessing.

Water buffaloes – locally known as Caribaos – haul cart loads of cane up to the railheads and the creatures could be seen intermittently appearing alongside the track. These buffaloes do marvellous work; their docile temperament rendering them ideal for long plodding cane hauls, though

Adventures at Ma Ao

periodically they like to rest submerged in water; only their noses and eyes appearing above the surface.

The train crew's company was very enjoyable; most knew some English and I was greatly entertained and completely at ease. Alongside one cane siding, grew several tall coconut trees and a brakeman asked me if I had ever tasted fresh coconut. My negative reply induced him to offer to obtain one. 'But how?', I asked, looking at the cluster of fruit 40 feet above us. 'By climbing the tree, master,' he grinned with a swarthy gold-plated smile, whereupon he shinned 35 feet up an almost smooth trunk to the leafy cluster containing the fruit. Three large coconuts landed with a 'thwack' alongside the engine. They were promptly chopped open and I was given the fresh cool milk to drink. Our final collection point was higher up the mountainside and it commanded an impressive view of the island; far below us in the distance could be seen the chimneys of Ma Ao factory.

With fifteen loaded trucks we began our descent; this time

running chimney first with the train behind us. Though little after 7.00 a.m., the heat quickly dispelled all memories of a cool night and, in accordance with custom, we had cut a supply of sugar cane to eat both for refreshment and energy during our journey. Little did I realise that I was soon to encounter the most terrifying experience of my life.

From my position on the tender I could look back along the train; our ambling pace generating a cool breeze. Suddenly I was shocked to see that we had become separated from our train and fifteen loaded sugar waggons were hurtling down upon the engine at great speed. I had been told of this happening many times often with terrible results as the waggons, upon striking the engine, frequently rear up over it; many deaths having been caused in this manner on industrial railways.

Flinging myself across the tender I screamed down to the driver; No.5 was blowing off, he did not hear. Expecting the crash any second and not daring to look behind me, I shouted down again in a voice I did not recognise as my own. I do not think he actually heard me, but some sixth-sense seemed to tell him what was wrong for, without turning round, he accelerated the engine with all the drama of a scene from 'The Great Locomotive Chase'. The rake was only feet away and still hurtling towards us, but our rapid acceleration prevented a serious collision and when it finally caught us up, all we felt was a gentle bump of couplings; No.5 quickly drew the train to a standstill.

The crew looked pale but I was actually shaking, so close had we been to a tragic accident. But such is human nature under adversity, that within seconds of halting we were all laughing as if it had been an act in a comedy show – one of the brakemen, who spoke a little English, did a hilarious mime depicting how the waggons might have ridden up over the engine and, drawing his finger across his throat, fell 'dead' to the ground. We soon discovered that a steel coupling pin, attaching the engine to the train, had snapped in half as if it were a matchstick. Presumably this had occurred when we had been hauling under stress; however the undulating track had enabled the engine to temporarily pull away on a short up-grade without anyone realising, but when the grade turned downwards again the train gained a terrific momentum – the engine meanwhile having slowed down on account of a particularly rough stretch of track. We replaced the pin from a reserve supply and continued our thenceforth uneventful journey back to the factory.

Plate 3 was made half an hour after the break-away happened.

Seven and a half hours after our departure we drew to a standstill in the factory yard. Our journey had been thrilling and although old No.5 had done it thousands of times before, even she must have breathed a sigh of relief to be back.

MA AO SUGAR CENTRAL –
ACTIVE STEAM ROSTER 1975

Engine Number	Wheel Arrangement	Builder	Date
BM 5	2–6–0	Alco (American Locomotive Company)	1924
TS 1	,,	,,	1921
TS 2	,,	,,	,,
TS 3	,,	,,	,,

All the above are ex Bacolod-Murcia Milling (now closed) or Talisay Silay Milling (largely diesel) – two factories from within the same company group. A pair of Ma Ao's indigenous Baldwin 0–6–2s are under repair. All other services are diesel.

16. Insular Lumber - a Legend!

Plates 4/5/6/17/19/21/22/34/45/46/52/55

Conrad emerged from the telephone office and, standing out-
lined against the light streaming through the doorway
called, 'No.7's within two kilometres.' This message heralded
the end of a 3 hour wait near the Insular Lumber Co.'s
(Ilco) coastal sawmill at Fabrica for the world's most incredible
steam survivor. The 3 hours were incidental, since I had waited
years to see this engine; years coloured by fears of her with-
drawal: at last the moment of truth had arrived. The crossing
gates over the Bacolod–Sagay road rattled down as a distant
whistle rang out like a cold shiver. The enormous mahogany-
burning Mallet – twice as large as I had imagined – eased
herself tender first over the crossing; I was spellbound by
the disjointed and freakish conglomeration of locomotion; she
was unique. The crossing lights revealed her faded green
livery lined in red, though her ornate eight-wheel bogie tender
was done in black with white letters pronouncing with gay
abandon, 'INSULAR LUMBER CO'; lesser scripts under-
neath proclaimed, 'no riders allowed'.

With mahogany sparks curling off her smokestack and
rasping steam from all cylinders, she clanked past with a long
trainload of log cars piled high with trunks eerily gliding
after her into the gloom. She stopped at the sawmill on a
ledge high above a huge artificial lake. The logs were to be
mechanically pushed from the waggons and allowed to
crash violently down a slope into the water below – known as
the log pan; from here a conveyor took them to the sawmill –
the logs being easier to process when wet.

From the opposite side of the lake, I watched No.7 ease a
log car into position and after grappling with it for a few
seconds the pusher dislodged an enormous trunk and sent
it thundering down into the pan. The ground shook under the
impetus and when the log finally hit the lake it sent a terrific

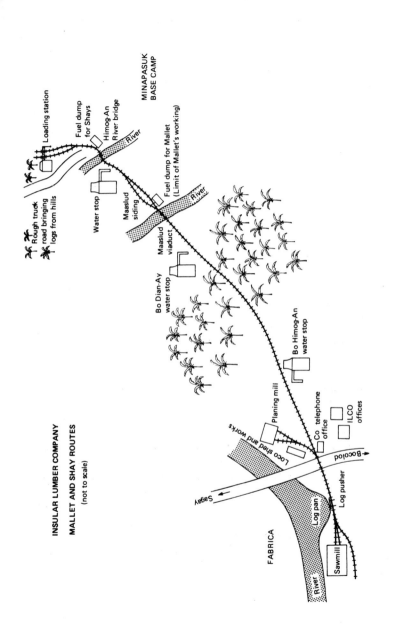

INSULAR LUMBER COMPANY

MALLET AND SHAY ROUTES

(not to scale)

Loading station

Rough truck road bringing logs from hills

Fuel dump for Shays

Himog-An River bridge

River

MINAPASUK BASE CAMP

Water stop

Maaslud siding

Fuel dump for Mallet (Limit of Mallet's working)

Maaslud viaduct

River

Bo Dian-Ay water stop

Bo Himog-An water stop

Planing mill

Co telephone office

Loco shed and works

ILCO offices

Sagay

Bacolod

Log pan

Log pusher

FABRICA

River

Sawmill

spray of water some 40 feet skywards. With three trunks sent down in rapid succession, No.7 drew her waggons forward emitting grotesque sounds from her four leaking cylinders; all of which had their valves out of alignment. Like an anguished creature she moved forward and back lit by sodium lights from the mill, her acrid silhouette was seen to be ever changing in ghostly patterns amid fire and swirling steam. After all logs had been ejected, she pushed the cars out of the mill. Each slip of a wheel obscured her in steam and produced a jet of crimson sparks accompanied by the most hideous sounds ever emitted from a locomotive: never had I heard or imagined an engine so haunted; the hollow rasps of her uneven exhaust might have been a ghost howling in hell.

Several derailments had occurred on the line that week and there were many logs to bring down; accordingly, the big Mallet prepared to return immediately up the line to Maaslud. Conrad was the company's engineer and rejoining him in the telephone office, I endeavoured to elucidate some information about No.7. I remarked upon the engine's haunting presence and he replied coolly; 'that engine has had a long and strange history. She was built by Baldwins in 1925, but I don't believe she came here new; it's said she came from neighbouring Cebu Island in the early '40s: I began here in 1946 – she was main line engine then! However, there is a retired employee living here in Fabrica who says he remembers No.7 arriving new in the 1920's – perhaps he's right – but I don't think anyone here today knows for certain.'

The train crews chatted about the Mallet's chequered life. She had been involved in more accidents and deaths than they cared to remember. They admitted frustration over the almost daily breakdowns and derailments, but the more serious disasters would remain in their minds forever. One night after heavy rains, No.7 started off a huge landslide as she rounded a hill; thousands of tons of earth and rock gave way under her and she rolled into a completely irretrievable position in a river bed far below. The Mallet had to be dismantled where she lay and the pieces hauled back up to track level by winching ropes; the wires used, can still be found to this day on the now overgrown hillside.

There were many other disasters. In September 1957, the veteran headed a train in which fifty people were killed when four log cars broke away from the rear of a loaded train coming down from Maaslud. Once the split had been noticed, the brakemen signalled the driver to stop; this he did on a high trestle bridge. But when the breakaway log cars caught up, they were travelling at high speed and, striking the train, they knocked it down into a ravine far below. Most of the dead were passengers illicitly riding the logs – hence the company's emblazoned slogan 'No Riders'.

As one of the enginemen put it, 'she is a ghost which refuses to die'. Kept going by ingeniously manufactured parts made in the company's workshop at Fabrica, Malley No.7 could, in her heyday, handle thirty-two, 30-ton log cars, but since her boiler pressure was reduced from 280 lbs per sq.in. to 220 lbs per sq.in., she has lost much power and, as the engine's condition causes concern, sixteen, 30-ton cars are now considered a maximum. Fortunately the decline in No.7's hauling abilities has been commensurate with a decline in log output from the mountain stands, much of the area already being cut out, and the company are now more concerned with their operation in the south where no railroad network is necessary. The system is already being run down; poor track over the 21-mile main line to Maaslud means that a journey takes over 6 hours, speed can rarely exceed 10 miles per hour.

After seeing the Mallet, one might assume that other engines would pale into insignificance, but the hideous looking Shays which ply their way between the sawmill and planing mill might be regarded by many as an even greater attraction. This is amongst the last of the Shay colonies in the world; the only others being at Lopez Sugar Central – just across the river from Ilco's sawmills – and on Taiwan's Ali Shan logging railway; Ilco's engines are, however, by far the best. Their improvised spark arresting chimneys, though quite ineffectual, are almost as high as the engines and include parts of cut-down oil drums. Another lovely Shay characteristic is their thick wooden buffer beams. These gorgeous chunks of Americana represent the last of a fascinating evolutionary variant upon the traditional steam locomotive.

The Shay, named after its designer Ephraim Shay, was a product of Lima Locomotive Works, Ohio; the first example appearing in 1880. Traditionally associated with America's Pacific Coast logging railways, the Shay saw little use elsewhere although some 2,700 examples are believed to have been built. The designer's object was to combine maximum power over steep gradients with an ability to traverse sharp curves and furthermore, to make the engine capable of running over hastily laid or indifferent quality trackbeds.

Shays are flexibly mounted on four wheel bogies known as 'Trucks'. The two-truck variety 'B' type, was the most common but three and even four truck examples were built; 'C' and 'D' types respectively; these additional units usually supporting a large tender. Unlike those of a conventional steam engine, a Shay's cylinders – usually two or three – are vertically mounted on the engine's right hand side, immediately in front of the cab. These drive a horizontal crank-shaft which via universal joints, traverses the engine's length incorporating all axles. This shaft carries pinions to engage with bevel gears on the wheels – an arrangement giving an easy turning movement (Plate 5). A Shay's boiler is rather delightfully displaced towards the left; a design feature necessary to offset the weight of cylinders and drive-shaft on the right (Plate 17).

Insular operate six Shays; three-cylinder 'B' types for the sawmills and larger three-cylinder 'C' types for tripping the mountain loading area – though one large Shay is kept in reserve to the Mallet for main line hauls. All are from Lima,

186

the oldest dating back to 1907 when the company first began.

Later that night, Lima Shay No. 10, a three-cylinder 'B' type, began tripping loads of planks from the sawmill up to the planing mill; a distance of about one mile. The whole town knew she was out on account of the fearsome racket she made. Shuffling along at a crawl, the engine ground and crashed its gears over the rickety metals and masses of flaming mahogany were flung 30 yards from the trackside – Plate 21 shows the scene. In 25 years of familiarity with engines, I have never found any so thrilling as those of Ilco. Several other Shays were working and collectively they produced a wide variety of whistles, both hooter and chime. Ilco's engines, more than any others, provided the idea for the title of this volume.

The logs are loaded in the mountains at Minapasuk – a remote community known within the company as Base Camp. As the mahogany stands have been progressively cut out, an ever lengthening road journey is necessary to reach the Minapasuk railhead. The big Shays trip the logs and empties over a 2 mile stretch to Maaslud sidings, where No. 7 takes over for the journey down to the sawmill; the track between Maaslud and the loading area being unsuitable for the 75-ton Mallet. Base Camp is a real backwoods community, isolated yet delightfully hospitable; a place where the aroma of woodsmoke drifting from the Shays mingles with the fragrance of 'native brewed' coffee stewing in wooden eating houses by the wayside. Logging is rough and dangerous work; accidents, derailments and mechanical problems assume nightmare proportions and the men, warm as they are in disposition, have inevitably acquired an aura of ruggedness.

During my time up at Base Camp, a typhoon struck and the rain lashed down for two whole days. The track disappeared under a sea of mud, yet the indomitable Shays, with all the pugnacity endorsed by their appearance, unstintingly went about their duties and continued whirring their way along at full throttle maintaining the usual 10 m.p.h. When the rain finally stopped, I ventured up to the loading area. The green clad mountains were bathed in a twilight mist and the huge trunks were piled up in a tangled mass starkly contrasting with the lifting gear. Standing in a quagmire of mud, I watched the twilight deepen and listened to the melodious whistle cry of Shay No. 12 on her way up from Maaslud. A chattering flurry from her pounding cylinders finally broke the silence as her bizarre shape emerged through the mists beneath a swirl of fire.

Throughout that night the old Shay worked logs to Maaslud and as we ran through leafy groves, spray from the wet branches cascaded down into the cab and provided refreshing relief from the footplate's clammy heat. The Mallet should have arrived soon after midnight, but had derailed en route. She arrived shortly before daybreak and so provided the ultimate spectacle of an original Baldwin 0–6–6–0 Mallet standing alongside a Lima Shay – as seen on Plates 19, 55; the two virile antiquarians in full blood with fiery stacks.

At dawn, Maaslud's inhabitants began to remove bark from the trunks since this is a useful domestic fuel and of no use to the company. Soon the stripped logs gleamed white, as can be seen by Plate 22 – made as Shay No. 12 gently backed the train up to where No. 7 was standing.

Jubilantly I set off for Maaslud's trestle viaduct situated half a mile down the line; here I was to picture the departing Mallet. A perfect morning had dawned with the distant mountain tops beautifully flecked with cloud. Sitting by that viaduct, I felt tense with excitement and when the Mallet eventually rounded the bend and eased on to the bridge, I experienced one of the greatest thrills of my life. Plate 52 shows the scene – 'a portrait of a dinosaur'.

The ecstasy of that long awaited moment was suddenly shattered when No. 7 ground to a halt on the bridge. The brakemen, whose job it is to ride the waggons and apply brakes as necessary during the descent, were frantically signalling to the

188

driver and pointing back along the train. Had a log shifted its position and threatened to fall into the river? Some minutes later the awful truth was realised; a brakeman had slipped on the wet trunks and fallen down into the abyss. Three long whistle blasts rang out from the Mallet – the disaster signal – and within seconds an answering call resounded over the groves indicating that Shay No. 12 was on her way.

Unconscious, the man was lifted back up to rail level and when Shay No. 12 arrived he was put on the foot plate and hurried round to an emergency hospital in Base Camp. After the log train had continued its precarious journey to the mill, it was found necessary to summon a diesel trolley up from Fabrica to take the injured brakeman to the main hospital there. Twelve kilometres down, the Mallet derailed herself bringing four log cars off with her – not surprisingly since in places the track was barely holding itself together. With the line well and truly blocked, the diesel trolley was unable to get through, thus an agonising delay of several hours occurred before the log train was rerailed and put into a loop. The trolley raced up to Base Camp followed by a wild dash down to Fabrica. Fortunately the man lived.

Never could I tire of that railway and its engines. I hope the accompanying plates capture something of the atmosphere for so much of the steam railway's romance seems epitomised at Ilco. The Mallet and Shay are swiftly fading into history, yet on this unique system, set in the finest of old American logging railway traditions, these relics steam on. They constitute a natural and perfect finale to *Iron Dinosaurs*.